THE
LOS ANGELES
HOUSE

TEXT AND
PHOTOGRAPHS BY

TIM
STREET-
PORTER

THE LOS ANGELES HOUSE

DECORATION AND DESIGN IN AMERICA'S 20TH-CENTURY CITY

CLARKSON POTTER/PUBLISHERS
NEW YORK

Published by Clarkson N. Potter, Inc., 201 East 50th Street, New York,
New York 10022. Member of the Crown Publishing Group.

Random House, Inc. New York, Toronto, London, Sydney, Auckland

CLARKSON N. POTTER, POTTER, and colophon are trademarks of
Clarkson N. Potter, Inc.

Manufactured in Japan

Design by Howard Klein with Renato Stanisic

Library of Congress Cataloging-in-Publication Data
Street-Porter, Tim.
The Los Angeles house: decoration and design in America's 20th-century
city / text and photographs by Tim Street-Porter.
1. Architecture, domestic—California—Los Angeles. 2. Interior decoration—California—Los Angeles—History—20th century. 3. Los Angeles
(Calif.)—Buildings, structures, etc. I. Title.
NA7238.L6S78 1995
728'.37'09797930904—dc20   94-23578 CIP

ISBN 0-517-70042-5

10 9 8 7 6 5 4 3 2 1

First Edition

ACKNOWLEDGMENTS

LOS ANGELES IS MANY THINGS TO MANY PEOPLE. To me, when I moved here some eighteen years ago, it was a visually stimulating urban environment. My compatriot, the artist David Hockney, felt the same way: it was a city of crisply defined architecture and palm trees, illuminated by a radiant light similar to that which had once attracted Van Gogh and Matisse to the South of France and Klee to North Africa.

This book is intended as a celebration of the best of Los Angeles, in this case its remarkable heritage of twentieth-century architecture and residential design, which provides an environment of unsurpassed richness and variety.

Many friends and colleagues have helped with the research and writing of this book, providing information and ideas and helping me gain access to particular houses. Tony Duquette has been a tireless inspiration. My gratitude also to Tom Hines, Hutton Wilkinson, Jeff Hyland, Ted Bosley, Tom Beeton, Ted Graber, Wallace Cunningham, Greg Padgett, Susan Heeger, Wallace Neff Jr., David Gebhard, John Chase, Robert Woolf, Hamish Bowles, Barry Sloane, Annie Kelly, and Made Wijaya.

Thank you to the staff of the excellent AGI Color Lab in Hollywood.

My thanks also to the staffs of the late, lamented *HG* and *LA Style* magazines, to the *Los Angeles Times* magazine, *Town & Country*, *W*, *Colonial Homes*, *World of Interiors*, and to others who have provided me with the opportunity to photograph some of the houses featured. These particularly include Elizabeth Sverbeyeff, Nancy Novogrod, Susan Goldberger, Jason Kontos, Susan La Tempa, Charles Gandee, Susan Zevon, Rochelle Reed, Barbara Thornburg, Beverly McGuire, Bill Swann, Rip Georges, and Beth Taubner.

I am indebted to the owners who generously allowed me to document their houses, making this book possible.

Special thanks go to my editor, Roy Finamore, who has a wonderful understanding of architecture and who undertook this project at such short notice.

CONTENTS

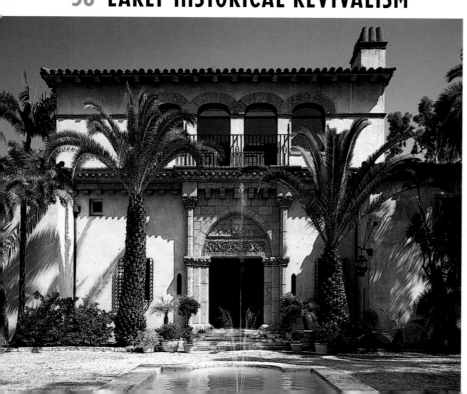

1

THE EVOLUTION OF THE LOS ANGELES HOUSE

OVER THE COURSE OF THE NINETEENTH CENTURY, the tiny settlement of El Pueblo de la Reina de Los Angeles grew into the moderately sized community of Los Angeles, with a population of 100,000. During the present century, however, the growth has been dramatic, and Los Angeles is now the nation's second largest cultural center. It can also be considered the country's quintessential 20th-century city.

Unlike most of the great cities of the Western world, which established themselves in previous centuries, L.A.'s rapid growth—the development of its sprawling suburbs and regional centers—has coincided with the advent of modern highways and transportation.

Los Angeles is a city where a Swiss chalet, a Colonial mansion, a Queen Anne cottage, and a Gothic castle can all be found on the same street. There is a popular theory to

PRECEDING PAGES: A swimming pool designed by Smith-Miller and Hawkinson, with landscaping by Akva Stein, overlooks the upper reaches of Beverly Hills. OPPOSITE: Lloyd Wright's dramatic 1926 Sowden house in Hollywood is built around an inner courtyard. THIS PAGE: 1. The Beverly Hills Robinson house, 1912, by Nathaniel Dryden. 2. Ornate 1920s apartments on Fountain Avenue in West Hollywood. They were designed by Meyer and Holler, architects of Grauman's Chinese Theater. 3. The 1898 Doheny house by Eisen and Hunt: a Spanish Gothic chateau built for oil tycoon Edward Doheny, in the then-fashionable enclave of Chester Place, near the downtown. 4. Made of river rock from the nearby arroyo, the Lummis house was built between 1898 and 1910 by Charles Lummis, an early champion of Mission-style architecture.

12 THE LOS ANGELES HOUSE

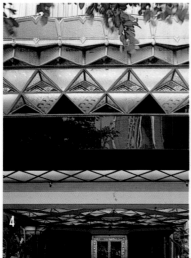

explain this spectacular variety: these many houses each represent the "big house" in the small town where the owner had grown up. Whether this town was back East, in Europe, or in the Far East, the intention was to provide a familiar refuge from a less-than-familiar world.

The result is a vast residential theme park. A drive through the hillsides and canyons of Beverly Hills, the Hollywood Hills, and Bel Air reveals a kaleidoscopic succession of vistas, exotic vegetation, and houses representing a bewildering range of styles and fantasies, pretensions, and idealistic visions. Nestled here are many of the country's most important examples of early Modernism.

The diverse architectural heritage of L.A. has not been influenced by the usual legacy of neoclassical architecture; the growth of the city is too recent. It has consequently followed its own unique path. Its residential design has been shaped by emotional concerns: by romance, by fantasy and a sense of freedom, by the city's wildly varied topography, and by the arrival of architects, primarily from Europe and the East Coast, who introduced both new movements in architecture and their own personal visions to the region.

The early settlers who flocked to California were inspired by reports of an undeveloped Eden on the shores of the distant Pacific. One of the catalysts was Helen Hunt Jackson's novel *Ramona*, published in 1881. An international best-seller, it portrayed the life of a beautiful half-Indian girl who grew up on a ranch near Los Angeles and created an irresistible

OPPOSITE: 1. "It's like swimming inside a wave," says owner Lynn Beyer of this John Lautner-designed swimming pool beside the beach in Malibu. 2. Robert Derrah designed the Coca-Cola bottling plant in downtown L.A. in the Streamline Moderne style to resemble an ocean liner. 3. Bridges link the street entry with each level of Brian Murphy's 1987 house for himself on Mesa Road in Santa Monica. 4. Designed for himself in a contemporary version of Spanish Colonial, the 1985 Barton Phelps residence spans a ravine in West L.A. 5. A colorful stand of Echium sastuosum—the Pride of Madeira—stands out against a mountain backdrop in the Taft botanical gardens near Ojai. 6. A view toward the swimming pool and house, from the garden of the Tony Duquette residence, Beverly Hills. THIS PAGE: 1. A glimpse of Lotusland in Montecito. The house, designed in 1920 by Reginald Johnson, is surrounded by giant cacti and euphorbia, part of the estate's exotic botanical gardens. 2. A 1920s adobe cottage, resembling a 19th-century rancho, near Ojai. 3. A 1930s Pueblo-Revival house in Santa Monica. 4. The lobby of the Art Deco Oviatt building, by Walker and Eisen, designed in 1927. 5. The elegant 1928 Villa d'Este apartments, by Pierpont and Walter Davis, in West Hollywood.

image of an undeveloped faraway land with a temperate Mediterranean climate, beautiful landscapes dotted with attractive Hispanic Mission-style buildings, and freedom from the constraints of Victorian society.

The reality, however, was a sparsely settled country of small pueblos and extensive ranchos. During the Spanish occupation, Franciscan monks, who arrived via Mexico, established a chain of twenty-one missions between San Diego and San Francisco. Both the missions and the simple houses built during this period were constructed with thick walls of sun-dried adobe bricks and roofs of handmade clay tiles. Their simple beauty and functionality inspired both the Monterey style of the mid-1800s and the subsequent Mission style, ancestors of the Spanish Colonial Revival style so evident in the late 1910s and '20s.

But not everyone who came to L.A. wanted to live like Ramona. Once a supply of wood became available from the north, a wider variety of styles was adopted. By the 1870s a succession of imported Greek Revival, Italianate, and Victorian styles—all highly decorated—had become popular. Most elaborate was the Victorian. Describing this, the architectural writer Ian Boyd White noted, "The Californian mix was much wilder, with the red bricks of Chelsea and the shingles of Newport, Rhode Island, jostled by a heady combination of domes, towers, pediments, floral and cactoid reliefs, and delicate wrought-iron works. It is the house that a committee made up of Genghis Khan, Leo Tolstoy, Victor Horta, and Norman Shaw might have dreamed up after a heavy night on piña colada!"

THIS PAGE: 1. A pergola in the Las Tejas estate in Montecito is supported by 15th-century French Romanesque columns. 2. Lautner's UFO-like Chemosphere house, 1960, built onto a steep slope near Laurel Canyon. 3. A Chinese-inspired bedroom in Tony Duquette's house in Beverly Hills. 4. A chair by Jon Bok with appliqued bottle caps against a textured wall in designer Larry Totah's Hollywood house. OPPOSITE: 1. An evocative court in the Bel Air Hotel, designed by Burton Scott in 1945. 2. Designed originally for a movie studio by Henry Oliver in 1921, the Spadena house—the ultimate Hansel and Gretel cottage—can be found in Beverly Hills. 3. A dovecote built into a corner of Wallace Neff's Millikan house, Pasadena, 1931. 4. The indoor pool at San Simeon, designed by Julia Morgan. 5. Apartments on Fountain Avenue in West Hollywood, designed by Arthur Zwebell in 1925. 6. Varied homes line the edges of the Venice Canal. 7. Paul Williams's 1950s redesign of the Beverly Hills Hotel facade. 8. Decorative ironwork in Wallace Neff's 1928 Collins house in San Marino.

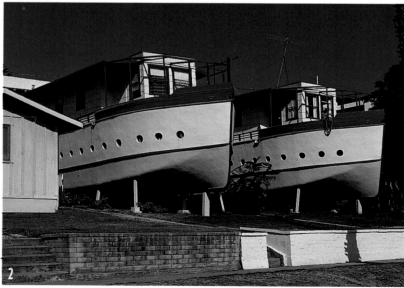

16 THE LOS ANGELES HOUSE

Stylishly renovated Victoriana can still be seen in profusion in Angelino Heights—the city's first suburb—particularly on attractive Carroll Avenue, a street where Victoriana is so pervasive that it is almost possible to experience a time warp (or at the very least to feel as if one is on a set from *Hello, Dolly!*). Angelino Heights is now a National Historic District with its own restoration foundation.

Early filmmakers discovered Los Angeles—and Hollywood—in their search for the combination of an agreeable climate and a wide variety of ready-made locations. The area's beaches, mountains, townscapes, jungles, and deserts were transformed into giant outdoor studios thanks to southern California's reliable sunshine.

The inspiration for much of L.A.'s scenographic architecture has been its resident movie industry. After the first foray by a film crew from Chicago in 1907, Hollywood quickly filled with production companies, and the sighting of downtown car chases and Western shoot-outs became a daily experience for Angelenos. Early structures—such as the immense ten-story Babylonian sets for *Intolerance,* which were erected at the junction of Hollywood and Sunset Boulevards in 1915 and remained in place for years—quickly became woven into the psyche of the city. These, combined with the early movie palaces and the glamorous movie-star homes of Mary Pickford and Douglas Fairbanks, Charlie Chaplin, Rudolph Valentino, and others, created a tension between fantasy and reality. Was a building real or was it a film set? Factories resembled Assyrian fortresses, and fast-food stands were surmounted by giant doughnuts large enough to be visible from the air.

OPPOSITE: <u>1</u>. El Molino Viejo, 1816, in San Marino. Now a museum, it was the first water-powered grist mill in southern California. <u>2</u>. Built in 1928, the SS Encinitas and the SS Moonlight are moored in a quiet street in Encinitas, near the beach, where they serve as rental condos. <u>3</u>.The garden of art collectors Clifford and Mandy Einstein's house in Brentwood, by architect Ron Goldman. The white structure is artist James Turrell's Second Meeting. THIS PAGE: <u>1</u>. Mandalay, 1953—the home of its creator, architect Cliff May, who was the pioneer of the ranch-style house. The rambling Mandalay is surrounded by courtyards, a dovecote, and sycamores. <u>2</u>. The 1885 Queen Anne-style Hale house, by Joseph Newsom, was rescued from demolition and moved to Heritage Square, off the Pasadena Freeway. <u>3</u>. A Spanish Colonial cottage in the Hollywood Hills is surrounded by a desert garden. <u>4</u>. A Brian Murphy-designed "picket fence" coffee table for a house in Santa Monica.

Then came Disneyland, an entire "magic kingdom" of fantasy architecture.

Dramatic variations in the city's topography also added to L.A.'s richly diversified architecture. Cities like Chicago, London, Paris, and New York all developed on predominantly flat land. Los Angeles offered a wide choice of topography—beaches, hills, ravines, plains—on which to build, necessitating equally varied responses from builders and architects. Rudolph Schindler, for example, who built on a variety of hillside lots, produced some of his best work on steep slopes, introducing stepped interlocking forms which added a sculptural complexity.

The ubiquitous California bungalow made an early appearance in the area. Climatically appropriate to the region, it was a one-story, loosely planned structure, dominated by an accommodating shallow-pitched roof with widely overlapping eaves. The broad sheltering roof resulted in verandas that ran the length of the house and provided sheltered living space. Although a little unprepossessing, the bungalow was cheap and could be ordered from a pattern book.

This was the first mass housing, a prototype for the suburban sprawl that was eventually to characterize Los Angeles, linked by the automobile and the freeway. It was an attempt to find a style that would reflect the region's relaxed, health-conscious lifestyle and its climate. And the Pasadena architects Greene and Greene finally gave the California bungalow an architectural pedigree.

OPPOSITE: **1**. A recent Lutyens-inspired courtyard and archway designed by Marc Appleton from an initial design by Tim Vreeland for Lily and Richard Zanuck frames a view of Beverly Hills. **2**. A dapper 1950s Regency-style house facade in San Marino. **3**. The house where Gloria Swanson lived while filming Sunset Boulevard is in a quiet corner of Whitley Heights. **4**. Designed by William Wurdeman and Welton Becket in 1935, the Pan Pacific Auditorium was the last word in Streamline Moderne. **5**. A courtyard in the Santa Barbara Mission. **6**. A cubistic house by Craig Hodgetts and Ming Fung overlooks a ravine in the Hollywood Hills. THIS PAGE: **1**. The courtyard of a 1920s Bel Air house by Roland Coate, decorated by owner Kathleen Spiegelman. **2**. This Assyrian palace, designed by Morgan Walls and Clements in 1929, was in reality a factory for the Samson Tire Company. **3**. South African aloes flower in the Taft gardens near Ojai.

THIS PAGE: <u>1</u>. House by Wallace Cunningham, 1990, in La Jolla. <u>2</u>. The courtyard linking the main house, left, with the studio at the 1949 Eames house, Santa Monica. <u>3</u>. The courtyard, with outdoor fireplace, at the Villa Vallombrosa, by Nathan Coleman, 1929. OPPOSITE: <u>1</u>. Frank Gehry's 1983 Norton house in Venice was built for an ex-lifeguard and featured a conceptual "lifeguard tower." <u>2</u>. Sunset at the Taft botanical gardens near Ojai. <u>3</u>. The back porch of Bette Midler and Martin von Haselberg's house in Bel Air. <u>4</u>. Disney's version of Hollywood decorating: Minnie Mouse's living room at Toontown. <u>5</u>.The front garden of a Beverly Hills house by Smith-Miller and Hawkinson. Landscaping by Akva Stein. <u>6</u>. Virtual reality: a suburban street created for the movie version of "The Flintstones" at Vasquez Rocks, near Los Angeles. <u>7</u>. Lloyd Wright designed this 1930s Mediterranean-Deco mansion in Holmby Hills. <u>8</u>. The romantic entry of the 1908 Gamble House, Pasadena, by Greene and Greene. The glasswork, depicting a live-oak tree, was designed by Charles Greene.

A NEW CENTURY

THE ARTS AND CRAFTS MOVEMENT emerged in England in the 1860s, a reaction to the effects of mass industrialization. Philosopher John Ruskin and designer William Morris advocated a return to craft techniques and the use of natural materials as an expression of a simpler, idealized way of life. The movement spread to the United States, first to Boston and Chicago. It became known as the Craftsman style, and it reached its fullest expression in the still-rustic environment of southern California, its arrival coinciding neatly with a reaction against the mad clutter of Victorian-style interiors.

In 1893, Charles Sumner Greene and Henry Mather Greene arrived in California. Recent graduates of MIT, they had been working in Boston when they decided to visit their mother in Pasadena. The town had become an important winter resort. It was newly linked with the East by railroad, which brought wealthy families like the Busches of St. Louis, the Wrigleys of Chicago, and the Gambles of Cincinnati. The most fashionable district was near the center of town, but a more adventurous group preferred the wild beauty of the nearby Arroyo Seco where, until a dam was built, boulders could be heard tumbling together after rainstorms. The Greene brothers were so impressed with the area that they opened an office there.

The Greenes were first inspired by the simplicity and honesty of the Franciscan missions, which linked northern California with Mexico. But their work evolved rapidly, and by 1902 a more recognizable Craftsman vocabulary began to show itself, with their design of the Culbertson house.

Here, for the first time, the Greenes collected rocks from the arroyo, which ran below the property, and applied them to the house's foundation and garden walls. Gray in color, they were combined with the rich russet and black tones of clinker blocks, creating a familiar design element which was known locally as the "peanut brittle" wall. With a low roof profile echoing that of the surrounding mountains, and the use of natural materials, the house responded both to the climate and to the rural nature of Pasadena. It set a standard for the high level of design that was to make the Greene brothers the most distinguished proponents of the Craftsman style in the United States.

The quiet, exclusive Pasadena enclave edged on two sides by the arroyo grew quickly during this first decade of the twentieth century to include the densest concentration of Greene and Greene houses to be found anywhere.

In 1892, a year before the Greene brothers traveled west, Irving Gill arrived in San Diego.

Oakholm, Charles S. Greene's own house in Pasadena, was built in 1901 and enlarged in 1906 to give additional studio space.

He had also worked for a brief period in the East and his lyrical response to new surroundings was recorded in *The Craftsman* magazine: "In California we have the great wide plains, arched blue skies that are chapters yet unwritten. We have noble mountains, lovely little hills and canyons waiting to hold the record of this generation's history, ideals, sense of romance and honesty."

He described the early adobes and the missions as "a most expressive medium for retaining tradition, history, and romance, with their long low lines, graceful arcades, tile roofs, bell towers, arched doorways, and walled gardens." Gill's locally imitated synthesis of the early mission architecture, as historian Esther McCoy has pointed out, gave San Diego the basis for what came close to being a regional style. Gill loved simplicity, and his pared-down version of Mission style prefigured Modernism.

The rugged, handcrafted Lummis house, finished in 1910, was built by Charles Lummis near the Arroyo Seco, a few miles downstream from Pasadena. Like the Greenes, Lummis used river rocks, giving the house the look of a rustic "folly."

Charles Lummis, with his magazine *Land of Sunshine,* was an enthusiastic promoter of the region's Hispanic heritage and a cofounder in 1894 of the California Landmark Club, one of the first preservation organizations in the United States. Their successful campaign to preserve the California missions resulted in the development of the popular Mission Revival style, which was adopted, complete with bell tower and domes, by the newly arrived Union Pacific Railroad for their train stations.

A wide variety of public buildings and houses were built in this style until 1915, when the Panama-California Exposition in San Diego introduced the immediately popular Spanish Colonial style, which was to dominate the region until the end of the 1920s. The advent of Spanish Colonial coincided with the demise of the Craftsman style. In 1915 Charles Greene moved to northern California, leaving his brother to continue the practice alone.

THE IRWIN HOUSE

BY GREENE AND GREENE

THE IRWIN HOUSE IS AN ENLARGED VERSION of the earlier Duncan house, built by the Greenes in 1900. At first it was a relatively simple one-story bungalow with a small interior courtyard. Built for Katherine Duncan, it presented little evidence of the distinctive Craftsman style which the architects were to introduce to the world three years later. Duncan did not enjoy the house for very long. After living most of her life in Pasadena she was suddenly smitten with a travel bug. She made a solo automobile trip across the country in 1903; three years later she sold the house and set off to Africa.

The new owner, Theodore Irwin, found the house too small and brought the Greene brothers back to add a second floor and upgrade the exterior in their new, fashionable Craftsman style. On the new upper floor the Greenes ran a balcony around the existing internal courtyard, covering the entire space with a protective pergola. This provided an intimate outdoor living area for the five bedrooms and billiard room that opened onto it: the attractive courtyard with its pool and fountain provided ventilation and light for the floor below.

The present owner, Michael Citron, has carefully restored the house, adding new wisteria-patterned stained-glass panels in the entrance, matching the vine that covers the pergola. The house is appropriately furnished with Craftsman furniture and a collection of California plein air paintings.

ABOVE: The welcoming entry of the Irwin house is protected by a roof canopy and a pergola of wisteria. The latter is depicted in the stained-glass entry panels designed by Michael Citron. OPPOSITE: The front terrace, separated from the lawn by a characteristic clinker-brick wall, enjoys a view of the arroyo and the San Gabriel mountains.

ABOVE: The dining room is furnished with reproduction Craftsman-style table and chairs. The overhead light fixture is original to the house. LEFT: The upper balcony was added to the enclosed courtyard in 1907. Shadows are cast from the overhead pergola. OPPOSITE: In the entry, a Harvey Ellis chair, a reproduction table, and a 1907 California plein air painting by Frederick Mulaupt welcome visitors.

THE GAMBLE HOUSE

BY GREENE AND GREENE

BUILT IN 1908, THE GAMBLE HOUSE represents the full flowering of the Craftsman period in this country. The house was designed by Greene and Greene, who felt it crucial that their houses be an overall craft statement and harmonious entity rather than a hollow architectural monument. The house is unique among houses by the Greene brothers in that it still contains the original custom-made furniture, fixtures, and accessories, which form an integral part of its design.

Approached by a sweeping drive, the house has a substantial scale that is modulated by its warm natural materials and the strongly expressed horizontality of its low-pitched roof planes with broad overhangs. A second-floor sleeping porch boldly projects from the northeast corner, balanced by a more traditional gable at the other end.

The striking entry hall has been lyrically described by several writers, most notably Reyner Banham and Charles Moore. It is a space that first welcomes, then causes a visitor to pause, momentarily overwhelmed by the beauty of the stained-glass door. Designed by Charles Greene, it depicts a California native oak of the kind found in the arroyo below.

In the early morning, the sunlight streaming through the east-facing fenestration is indeed beautiful, transforming the space, in Banham's words, into "an Aladdin's cave or a sacred grove." Once the initial moment of transcendence has passed, this space can be seen as a low-ceilinged entry hall of generous proportions, a marshaling point before venturing further. The walls and staircase are of hardwood, rubbed and softened so that they appear—and feel—as smooth as velvet. The carefully articulated design and detailing of the staircase, inspired by Japanese joinery, is typical of the care that has infused the whole house.

With its various nooks and recesses, the living room invites a variety of activities. The fireplace occupies an alcove spanned by a massive truss of Burmese teak. Inglenooks face each other across the fireplace, which is decorated with tiled panels inset with a mosaic of iridescent glass and tile depicting a trailing vine. On the opposite side of the room, another alcove, echoing the first, projects out into the rear terrace overlooking the garden and the arroyo below.

The dining room is executed with similar care, incorporating its specially made furniture and lamps into a single unified design. Windows behind the built-in cabinet depict blossoming vines in leaded glass. The kitchen opens onto a screened porch—the servants' dining area—and both are filled with sunshine all day. Upstairs, the family rooms are light in tone and mood. Each bedroom extends out to its own terrace or sleeping porch. These were considered healthy for year-round sleeping (remember, this was a time when the air was drier and permeated with the scent of orange blossom rather than traffic fumes). They are sheltered and protected by broad balustrades with Japanese-inspired joinery detailing and massive overhead beams.

This house, which joined several earlier Greene and Greene houses in the same quiet enclave adjacent to the arroyo, is on the National Register of Historic Places and is open to the public on specific days each week. Exquisitely preserved, and with all its furnishings intact, it remains a remarkable record of an earlier golden age of Californian design.

Stepping stones, part of the Greenes' original design for the Gamble house, lead to the rear of the house, which rests on a gentle swell of lawn. Low-pitched roofs, broad eaves, and sleeping porches give the house a horizontally expressed silhouette, echoing the rolling nature of the terrain.

RIGHT: An interior stained-glass window, designed by Charles Greene. BELOW: The light-filled kitchen received the same attention to detail as the rest of the house. The staff quarters can be seen through the doorway. OPPOSITE, CLOCKWISE FROM TOP: The focal point of the living room is the fireside inglenook, with mahogany furniture designed by the Greenes for the house. As elsewhere in the house, the mahogany beams over the inglenook were hand-rubbed to a velvety smoothness. The dining room is another example of the Greenes' integrated approach to design: the furniture, the lamp fixture, and the stained-glass window behind the rear counter were all designed for the house.

ABOVE: A bird's-eye maple desk and chair are set in the corner of the guest bedroom.
LEFT: The light-toned guest bedroom is situated on the ground floor, near the entrance.
The beds—made of nickle-plated brass and designed for the house—are one example
of the Greenes' readiness to experiment with new materials. The rocking chair is made
of bird's-eye maple.

THREE HOUSES

BY IRVING GILL

THE MILTIMORE HOUSE WAS BUILT IN 1911 in a verdant South Pasadena neighborhood that was once occupied by a forest of California live oaks. Several of these trees remain in the middle of the street facing the Miltimore house, and the front garden remains a dense oak grove.

The architect of this house was unknown until its owner recognized a window detail from an article on Gill by architectural historian Esther McCoy. After some research, McCoy established that this was indeed a Gill house.

The Morgan house dates from 1917. Built entirely of concrete near Melrose Avenue in Hollywood, it is a single-story structure entered from the side through a courtyard, with an arched opening at each end. The house is simple, but various design features give it added character. The interior has high ceilings with additional light entering from narrow clerestories. The central courtyard, literally an outdoor room, is partly sheltered and can be used as a sleeping porch. The concrete floor devised by Gill was specially prepared by adding pigment so that its rich tones matched rugs and furniture and, when waxed like hardwood, gave an effect of old Spanish leather.

Discovered by furniture designer Roy McMakin, the house has been painstakingly renovated and restored to its original condition. False ceilings and partitions were removed; concrete walls were sandblasted and painted white. The window trim was returned to the dark blue-green favored by Gill. McMakin, using his own furniture combined with carefully chosen found pieces, has furnished the house in a way that respects its spirited astringency as well as Gill's pared-down pre-Modernist sensibility.

The architecturally striking Horatio West Court was designed in 1919 and sits on a quiet street close to the oceanfront in Santa Monica. A few years ago a group of architects bought the dilapidated apartment complex and restored it to its original condition.

The apartments are built around a central patio. They feature sunny upstairs living rooms with glazing that wraps around on three sides, giving views of the ocean and the mountains.

ABOVE: The Miltimore house, seen here in front elevation, emerges from a grove of live oaks. OPPOSITE: The wisteria-draped pergola is stripped of ornament—a revolutionary idea at the time of its construction.

LEFT: Morgan house, Hollywood, 1917. Owner Roy McMakin has restored the internal courtyard, placing a daybed of his own design below the sheltering roof overhang.
BELOW: The entry courtyard of the Morgan house is framed by an arch, the only curved form to appear in Gill's rigorously cubistic designs of this period. OPPOSITE: Horatio West Court, Santa Monica, 1919. Gill's design for this compact 4-unit complex anticipates the International Style architecture of the 1920s.

EARLY HISTORICAL REVIVALISM

THE CHIEF DESIGNER AT THE 1915 Panama-California Exposition in San Diego was the distinguished New Yorker Bertram Goodhue, who had traveled in Mexico, preparing drawings for a book on Mexican architecture. His buildings for the exposition were modeled on Mexican baroque church design, with flamboyant churrigueresque flourishes. The Spanish Colonial style introduced by this exposition soon had a huge impact on the region's cultural and physical landscape. It is required by code in some outlying cities and historic neighborhoods of Los Angeles.

By contrast, Modernism has always been a minority taste in L.A.'s residential areas. Unlike Mexico City, where more than 80 percent of houses in the wealthier suburbs are in the Modernist tradition, L.A. has turned to revived historical styles for most of its housing. The most refined proponents of early Historical Revivalism, from 1915 until its decline around 1930, were George Washington Smith, Wallace Neff, Roland Coate, and John Byers. Smith worked prolifically in Santa Barbara and nearby Montecito from 1919 until he died in 1930. He initially studied architecture but became an artist instead, studying and working in Paris and New York. He then moved to Montecito in 1916 in order to paint.

Like Pasadena, Montecito—and nearby Santa Barbara—had become a popular winter resort for well-to-do easterners. Its physical characteristics and orientation led Baedeker in 1893 to describe it as "America's Menton," sharing as it did with the popular French resort a perfect orientation toward south-facing beaches, and it was similarly backed by a coastal range of mountains. Smith was charmed by the area and built himself a house. It was so well received that he was encouraged to open an architectural office in 1919. "I soon found that people were not really as eager to buy my paintings, which I was laboring over, as they were to have a whitewashed little house like mine."

During his brief but prolific career, Smith built a considerable number of houses and public buildings. This legacy was instrumental in establishing Santa Barbara as the preeminent Spanish Colonial city in California. Resident historian David Gebhart has noted "the really unique aspect of Santa Barbara and its environs is that man's manipulation of this place has, on the whole, enhanced rather than devastated it." During the 1920s his reputation spread quickly, and he was invited to design houses in Los Angeles for Samuel Goldwyn and Mary Pickford and Douglas Fairbanks.

Modeled on the designs of Andalusian farmhouses and country estates taken from the books that were available at the time, Smith's work was characterized by a spareness of form and roof line and a richness of detail and material. When grander houses were required, Smith turned to the designs of Italian villas. But his houses invariably reflected a concern for fastidious craftsmanship and subtlety of design.

Smith designed intimate patios, outdoor rooms that established a close link between the house and the garden. Thanks to his demand for appropriate detailing, local craftsmen were soon producing attractive ceramic tiles and delicate wrought ironwork.

The fascination with Spanish Colonial design reached its zenith during the 1920s, continuing the myth

Las Tejas, Montecito, designed by Francis Wilson in 1927 and redecorated by John Saladino in 1990 with fresco wall-treatments by Christian Granvelle.

of Los Angeles as a Mediterranean paradise. City halls, businesses, apartment buildings, even gas stations conformed to a romantic Hispanicism. There were housing developments such as Whitley Heights and Hollywoodland, city centers in Brentwood, Westwood Village, and Pacific Palisades, all contributing to an indigenous look that was functionally and climatically appropriate.

Wallace Neff, another distinguished Revivalist, began his practice in 1923. He studied at MIT and was most prolific during the 1920s. His most famous house—but by no means his best—was Pickfair, built for Mary Pickford and Douglas Fairbanks and recently demolished by Pia Zadora.

Neff was the most evocative of historicist architects, with a sense of the picturesque, and his buildings were the most widely copied. He possessed an exquisite sense of line: his roof profiles are delicately continued to the ground, either with extended articulated walls or, in the case of his Normandy houses, with the steep stylized line of the roof itself, which swoops down to graze the landscaping. Sadly, the best features of many of Neff's greatest houses are today obscured by foliage (or "shrubbed up," in the words of Wallace Neff Jr., his father's archivist), and remodeled beyond recognition.

Historical Revivalism was not popular with everyone in the 1920s, however. Frank Lloyd Wright, busy with his vision of appropriate contemporary architecture, spoke scornfully of "tawdry Spanish medievalism" and its "flatulent or fraudulent lack of identity."

CASA DEL HERRERO

BY GEORGE WASHINGTON SMITH

CASA DEL HERRERO (HOUSE OF THE BLACKSMITH) is one of George Washington Smith's most evocative houses, designed in a Spanish Revival style with Moorish details. Built for the Steedman family between 1922 and 1925, it was finished a few days before a devastating earthquake, which it survived unscathed.

The north facade confronts a stone-paved entry courtyard with a central fountain. The composition of this elevation, with its highly abstracted asymmetry, is typical of the sophisticated Andalusian style. The east elevation opens onto a patio, which functions as an outdoor room. This attractive space is filled with morning light and is linked to a series of Moorish gardens. A loggia set into the south facade opens onto an extensive lawn, which directs the eye down a slight slope toward the sea. Recycled water flows from a small tiled pond set in the grass to an Alhambra-influenced water channel leading to a series of tiny fountains. A shady paved area with a final raised fountain terminates the vista, beyond which a low wall and gate open onto a desert wilderness garden.

The house has been occupied by a single family since the 1930s, and the decoration dates back to this period. Much of the furniture is Spanish antique: an atmospheric evocation of dark wood chairs and tables, with rich brocades and leather upholstery. Rooms are cool and dark, decorated with religious statues and attractive imported tile.

TOP: The Andalusian-style facade of Casa del Herrero faces a stone-paved courtyard and tiled fountain. ABOVE: A garden view of the house with its recessed loggia. Water circulates from a star-shaped pool set into the lawn into a channel inspired by one in the Alhambra in Spain. OPPOSITE: The water flows down a gentle slope from the house and terminates in a shady, tiled fountain.

ABOVE AND OPPOSITE: A gate, just below the fountain, leads into a lower "wilderness" desert garden dominated by a stand of dragon trees (Dracaena draco). The walls are decorated with locally produced tile. LEFT: This detail of the front facade shows the hand-finished stucco and tile work, a typical feature of houses from the period.

OPPOSITE, CLOCKWISE FROM TOP: The living room's carved woodwork and antique furniture evoke ancient Spanish interiors; the door at left opens onto a patio. An antique tapestry greets visitors in the entry hall. The patio outside the living room catches the morning light and serves as an outdoor room. LEFT: The fireplace and deep window reveal in this bedroom are inspired by similar treatments in Andalusian farmhouses. BELOW: A staircase rises gently from the dining room, furnished with 18th-century European dining table and chairs.

THE HUNTINGTON ESTATE

BY MYRON HUNT
GARDENS BY HENRY HUNTINGTON
WITH WILLIAM HERTICH

THE HUNTINGTON ESTATE WAS CREATED as a retirement home by businessman Henry Huntington and his wife, Arabella. Huntington was an urban planner whose company, the Pacific Electric Railway, established L.A.'s interurban rail system, the world's largest at the time, and helped facilitate the region's prodigious growth in the early decades of the century.

Between them, the couple amassed important collections of rare books and English art. Both are housed in galleries and in the library, which form a nucleus of buildings around the mansion itself. The mansion was designed by architect Myron Hunt in 1910.

The most visible legacy of the Huntingtons' collecting instincts is to be found in the 207 acres of gardens surrounding the house. Together with his remarkable assistant, William Hertich, Huntington created one of the nation's most important and extensive botanical gardens, with specimens, often full-grown, brought in with great difficulty and perseverance from all corners of the world.

The gardens are arranged as a series of zones around a central English lawnscape in front of the main house. A long trellised path leads off in one direction to the Japanese garden, separating the encyclopedic rose garden from the Shakespeare garden (filled with herbs mentioned in the plays). There are important gardens of cycads, camellias, palms, and other tropical plants, and a large, less-defined zone of Australian flora.

Most remarkable of all, however, is the twelve-acre desert garden, the largest and most comprehensive collection of desert plants in the world. Planted on arid, south-facing slopes where nothing else would grow, the collection has thrived and matured for nearly a century and has created a landscape resembling the world of science fiction more than that of conventional horticulture.

ABOVE: A pergola leads visitors through the rose garden, toward the Japanese garden and other wonders on the estate. OPPOSITE: Designed by Myron Hunt and Elmer Grey in 1910, the current art gallery (originally the house) sits facing a broad expanse of lawn and trees.

ABOVE: The lawns below the art gallery are punctuated by a small classical temple.
OPPOSITE: To the north of the gallery, an avenue of grass—framed by rows of 18th-century French statuary, camellias, and palms—terminates in a large fountain and view of the San Gabriel mountains (not seen in the photograph). FOLLOWING PAGES: The desert garden—with the largest collection of desert plants in the world—is set on twelve acres. Many of the specimens were already mature when they were laboriously transported to the site more than eighty years ago. Pathways through the desert garden seemingly transport the visitor to a distant planet.

THE MOSQUE HOUSE

ARCHITECT UNKNOWN

WITH ITS COLORFUL MINARETS, DOMES, and fortified parapets, this late-1920s Islamic fantasy conjures visions of Morocco. Overlooking Silver Lake Reservoir, it is a charming example of the spirit of fantasy architecture that flourished in L.A. during this period.

Built into a steep hillside, the house is on four levels and is larger than its cottagey interior spaces suggest. Rooms open onto a variety of balconies, patios, and terraces at different levels, each with a sun-filled view of the lake, hills dotted with houses, and the San Gabriel mountains beyond.

The house has been completely restored. The current owner added new tilework and painted decoration and filled the interior and exterior spaces with his collections of early California pottery. The furniture is eclectic, with newly added Moroccan tables and Persian carpets contributing to the Oriental aura.

RIGHT, FROM TOP: The exterior of the 1920s Mosque house overlooks Silver Lake Reservoir. A shady patio and fountain. A view of the Silver Lake hills from a Moorish archway outside the living room. OPPOSITE: The ceiling of the dining room, with a lantern suspended from a brightly painted ceiling recess, evokes a giant flower hovering over the table.

THE ADAMSON HOUSE

BY STILES CLEMENTS

OCCUPYING A LOW SANDY HEADLAND, with a view of Santa Monica Bay and the pier beyond as well as the Malibu Lagoon Wildlife Sanctuary, the Adamson house enjoys one of the few genuinely pretty sites on the Malibu coast. Set in an attractively landscaped garden, the house represents Spanish Colonial Revival architecture at its most picturesque.

Designed in 1929 by Stiles Clements, of Morgan Walls and Clements (the architects responsible for many of L.A.'s most evocative landmark buildings, including the Wiltern, Mayan, and El Capitan Theaters, as well as the exotic Babylonian fortress–style Richfield Tire Plant), the house was built as a beach residence for Rhoda Rindge and her husband, Merritt Adamson, founders of Adohr Farms (*Adohr* is *Rhoda* spelled backward). Her father, Frederick Rindge, owned a 17,000-acre ranch that included most of today's Malibu; at the time the house was built, the family owned everything the eye could see. In the late 1920s, thanks to Malibu's reputation as a fisherman's paradise, the Rindges leased plots of land to Ronald Coleman, Buster Crabbe, Harold Lloyd, and other Hollywood actors, creating the nucleus of what was to become the Malibu movie colony.

The Malibu Potteries Tile Company—a company owned by the Rindge family—supplied the colorful tiles that are recognizable to anyone who has visited old and unrenovated kitchens and bathrooms in southern California. It is the extent of this tilework that makes the Adamson house unlike any other. A showplace for the family's products, the house exudes color and pattern from every interior and exterior surface. Each room has its own theme. The kitchen reflects native American influences, while the bathrooms are covered from floor to ceiling with tile depicting flowers and plants visible on the property. The real tour de force, however, occurs in the loggia, with its tiled, trompe l'oeil Persian rugs, complete with a fringe at each end, designed by potter William Handley.

The furnishings are in a Spanish style and were designed for the house, except for a fine French antique table and a Farsi prayer rug that hangs in the loggia. The interior designer, John Holtzclaw, hired Danish artists Ejnar Hansen and Peter Nielson (who also worked on L.A.'s Biltmore Hotel) to add decorative painting to many of the interior surfaces. Beams, ceilings, doors, and walls are adorned with an outpouring of Scandinavian and Hispanic folk-art motifs.

The Adamson family made the house their permanent home in 1936. Following the death of Rhoda Rindge Adamson in the late 1960s, it was left to the state of California. The decision to bulldoze the house to provide a parking lot for beachgoers was prevented by the hastily formed Malibu Historical Society, which took the state to court and won. The house is now represented on the National Register of Historic Places and is open to the public. It is one of the best-loved houses in southern California.

ABOVE: Beyond the "Peacock Fountain," the lawn stretches to meet the ocean. Malibu Pier can be glimpsed in the background. OPPOSITE: The east facade of the Adamson house. The big arched window of the dining room is to the right. Behind the patio, where the Peacock Fountain is located, is the loggia. The main living room is to the left, and beyond this is the ocean.

ABOVE: The dining room table—one of the house's few antiques—is French. Plaster ceiling panels are painted to resemble wood; the stepped edges are gold-leafed. Both the Belgian linen draperies and the chandelier are original to the house. LEFT: The kitchen is dramatically tiled. Orange flower patterns echo those of a coral tree outside. The inset clock is hinged for resetting. The tiled floor patterns are repeated in the ceiling's paintwork. Beyond the door is the dining room.

OPPOSITE: The loggia is dominated by an extraordinary trompe l'oeil Persian carpet of tile, designed for the house by William Handley. LEFT: An electric clock and tiled table were both designed for the house's entry hall. The dining room can be seen through the arch. BELOW LEFT: High-quality iron and tilework—seen here in the stairway—are a feature throughout the house. BELOW: The nurse's room includes a pair of beds made especially for the house.

CASA BIENVENITA

BY ADDISON MIZNER

ADDISON MIZNER WAS BORN IN SAN FRANCISCO, but his working life was spent on the East Coast. There he was best known for literally setting the style for the resort development of Florida. Based in Palm Beach during the 1920s, Mizner designed luxurious houses, clubs, and public buildings, all in a distinctive Mediterranean style and embellished with decorative elements produced in his own workshop or plundered from ancient buildings in Europe.

The enchanting Casa Bienvenita in Montecito was the only house he built in his home state. East Coast businessman Alfred Dieterich first visited Santa Barbara in 1915 and bought sixteen acres in Montecito a few years later. Mizner, who had built a previous house for Dieterich in Millbrook, New York, was a natural choice to design the new house.

The house is U-shaped, surrounding three sides of a cloistered patio furnished with palms and an ornamental pond. This sunny, perfectly scaled outdoor living area is the heart of the house, its brightness filtering into the dark recesses of the surrounding interior spaces.

Mizner designed Casa Bienvenita in a typically eclectic style, with Spanish, Moorish, Gothic, Romanesque, and Renaissance influences. As with most of his houses, he used cast-stone decorative elements, including door and window surrounds, all manufactured in his Florida studios.

The house has a formal entry; a flight of steps leads up into a massive vaulted space, part hallway and part cloister, with the courtyard to the left and the main living room to the right.

The large hanging lanterns appear to have been made in Mizner's studios, but many of the doors throughout the house are trophies from Mizner's annual buying trips to Italy and Spain. The living room versions are particularly elaborate, carved with the figures of saints and popes.

Robert Woolf, a decorator and the adopted son of Los Angeles architect John Woolf, bought the house in 1979. It was in surprisingly good condition, despite having received no maintenance for twenty years. Under his careful eye the house and gardens have been restored to their original spirit. Woolf painted the walls a rich coral, using a paler tone for the hallways. This gave the house a much-needed warmth. He furnished Casa Bienvenita mostly with furniture from his earlier house, although he was left some pieces by the previous owner. Both cloisters are lined with original sliding glass panels to protect the interiors from cold weather. These are framed by cast columns in pairs—set inside and outside the glass to provide both interior and exterior decoration. The living room—with its deeply coffered ceiling and a fireplace that Mizner brought from a château in the Pyrénées—is a grand space, looking out to an extensive lawn and trees. Sunny lemon yellow is the color Woolf chose for the main bedroom. Dominated by a Venetian chandelier, original to the house, the room opens to fine views of the rose garden.

Much work was done restoring the sadly neglected gardens, designed by Mizner himself. More than 1,200 new rosebushes were planted to replace the old dead ones, and there is once again a vegetable garden. Dense undergrowth, which obscured the vista to the teahouse, was cleared away, and the hedges flanking the rose garden were cut back to reveal double rows of cast spiral columns that match the spiral motif of the chimneys.

Casa Bienvenita was one of Mizner's last houses (he died in 1933) and is probably one of the best still in existence (many of his larger Florida villas were torn down by developers in the 1950s). This substantial commission was welcome and timely, as by 1928 the Florida real estate boom was winding down and Mizner's career had consequently slowed almost to a standstill.

The front facade of Casa Bienvenita is decorated with cast-stone elements that were fabricated at Mizner's workshops in Florida.

ABOVE: Placed on an axis with the house's central patio, steps lead up from a formal flagstoned court to a circular fountain flanked by Italian Renaissance urns. From here, an Italianate vista garden, with twin water cascades and edged with cypress, ends with a tea pavilion. RIGHT: Statuary and eucalyptus mingle gracefully on the garden terrace.

LEFT: Surrounded on three sides by the house, the cloistered patio functions as an outside room and serves as the central focus of the house. BELOW: The balcony of the master bedroom overlooks the rose garden, which was designed by Mizner and restored by the current owner. To the left is the garden terrace.

ABOVE: The east cloister enjoys a view of the central patio, seen through double columns set on either side of sliding glass panels. The Pompeian figures are terra-cotta. The breakfast table is used for most informal meals. ABOVE RIGHT: The entry cloister, with vaulted roof, looking toward the entrance. A glazed metal door to the central patio is to the right, and the door to the living room can be seen on the left. The lanterns are from the Mizner studio. RIGHT: Woolf chose a sunny lemon-yellow for the master bedroom. Dominated by a Venetian chandelier (original to the house), the room opens to fine views of the rose garden. OPPOSITE: The living room—with its deeply coffered ceiling and an 18th-century fireplace that came from a chateau in the Pyrénées—looks out to an extensive lawn and trees. The ceiling is similar to those Mizner designed for several houses in Palm Beach.

CONSTANTIA

BY AMBROSE CRAMER

ARCHITECT AMBROSE CRAMER DESIGNED CONSTANTIA in 1930 for an executive of the Armour company. The style is Cape Dutch, evidently inspired by one of Cecil Rhodes's houses in Capetown, South Africa. Six attractively scrolled gables, a feature of this style, accommodate the steep pitches of the roof.

The gardens were landscaped by Lockwood de Forest to make the most of a modest-sized lot (by Montecito standards). The north-facing living room nonetheless overlooks one of the grandest views in Montecito: a vista of reflecting pools, fountains, and a colony of black swans, with the mountains beyond.

ABOVE AND OPPOSITE: From the living room and adjacent terrace there is a spectacular view of swans, water, trees, and mountains. LEFT: One of the scrolled gables, characteristic of the house, frames the entry. TOP: Ornate candelabra and an antique chest provide a taste of the interior furnishings.

THE VILLA VALLOMBROSA

BY NATHAN COLEMAN

THE VILLA VALLOMBROSA IS SET INTO a steep hillside above a tiny hidden valley in Whitley Heights, a planned Spanish Colonial Revival development typical of the 1920s. A walk around the area reveals a charming network of narrow streets, each house carefully positioned with a view over its neighbor.

Many stars of early Hollywood were drawn to this stylish new development, which is now a National Historical Monument, among them Valentino and Chaplin (whose houses were torn down to make way for the Hollywood Freeway), Gloria Swanson, Carole Lombard, William Powell, and Maurice Chevalier.

The Villa Vallombrosa has a rich history typical of Hollywood. Greta Garbo used to dine with Adrian in the courtyard (he was designing the costumes for *Mata Hari* at the time, and lived in the villa between 1932 and 1934), and a self-portrait by the celebrated fashion photographer Baron de Meyer, taken in front of the fireplace, sits in the same room.

The villa typifies the strong element of fantasy found in Hollywood in 1929. With its curved facade and single long window like an exclamation point, the house evokes a palazzo on the Grand Canal in Venice, or a small villa in Tuscany.

The front door opens into a tiny vestibule from which tunnellike stairs curve theatrically upward to explode into the twenty-foot-high sitting room on the *piano nobile*. At the far end of the room, arched French doors open onto a small, enclosed courtyard separated from the hillside garden by a high wall topped with stone urns. This outdoor room, complete with a fireplace, is enclosed on the other three sides by the house itself and overlooked by a *Romeo and Juliet* bedroom balcony. The tinkle of a fountain and the courtyard's feeling of enclosure give a sense of isolation from the city.

The villa was designed by architect Nathan Coleman, who had already built several houses in the area for Mrs. Eleanor de Witt, a woman of great character and personality. She wanted a retreat from the winters of the East Coast, but she decided to move in permanently after the house was completed and lived there more or less (leasing it on occasion) until her death in the late 1950s.

Several years ago the villa was bought by me and my artist-designer wife, Annie Kelly. We have furnished it as much as possible in the style it was intended to embody, with a nostalgic sense of old Europe evident in period furniture, wall hangings, and textiles. Fortuny fabric is used throughout the house, a re-creation of old Venetian fabric that expresses the same nostalgia for the past.

ABOVE: Behind the villa is a steep garden with a view of Whitley Heights beyond.
OPPOSITE: The Venetian-style facade, with its original, unpainted cement stucco.

OPPOSITE: The window looks out onto the park surrounding the Hollywood Bowl. The drawing-room curtains are of parchment-colored silk; the chair is 19th-century American Gothic. BELOW LEFT: The "Romeo and Juliet" living room balcony overlooks the front terrace. BELOW: The Italian-made lamp over the entry is original to the house.

ABOVE: The mirror, sconces, and chairs in the living room are all 19th-century French. The coffee table, supported by crossed spears, is Mexican. ABOVE RIGHT: An 18th-century embroidered panel hangs on the twenty-foot-high walls, which cove seamlessly into the ceiling. The lamp is an 18th-century altar candlestick. RIGHT: In a corner of the drawing room, Kelly's partially mirrored folding screen underscores the Venetian Gothic style of the house.

ABOVE: A silk-swagged French window opens to a balcony festooned with honeysuckle and overlooking the central courtyard. The Fortuny fabric on the armchair matches the silver-brown damask of the wallpaper. The chandelier is from the 1920s, the same period as the house. ABOVE RIGHT: A Mexican painting of a Madonna and Child hangs over a Directoire sofa and a table by artist Jim Ganzer. RIGHT: The candlelit dining room is glimpsed from the central courtyard.

CASTILLO DEL LAGO

BY JOHN DELARIO

BUILT IN THE 1920S BY ARCHITECT JOHN DELARIO, Castillo del Lago sits serenely on its promontory above Hollywood Lake, with unrivaled views of the L.A. basin.

Occupied for a while by Bugsy Siegel (there are rumored to be bullet holes in the entry hall's woodwork), Castillo del Lago has become the stylish home of the singer and actress Madonna, with renovations and decorations by her brother, artist-decorator Christopher Ciccone.

The house, which was previously white, has attracted attention with its new bold colors. The oxblood red of Castillo del Lago, and its bold stripes, represent a departure for a city which, compared to Miami or Mexico, is chromatically conservative. Ciccone, who was inspired by a similarly striped church in Positano, Italy, remembers his early impressions of the house and its setting: "It just felt like Italy here, in every aspect." Since striping of this kind and in the same colors is also a tradition in certain Umbrian villages, Ciccone's embellishments provide an enrichment to the area's Mediterranean heritage.

Ciccone (who has collaborated with Madonna on previous projects) felt that the interiors, with their beamed ceilings and ornate detailing, "needed something very rich and of high quality. There just didn't seem to be other options." The rich reds of the living room and the bold use of stripes in the bedrooms; the liberal use of brocades, silks, and velvets; and the high-quality antiques all suggest opulence, but with a light touch. To offset the richness of the furnishings, Ciccone painted the interior walls an austere white.

TOP: South view of Castillo del Lago, overlooking Griffith Park. ABOVE: The east elevation of the house faces a lawn and pool, as well as spectacular views of the city. OPPOSITE: Castillo del Lago sits serenely on a hilltop overlooking Hollywood Lake, a reservoir built and landscaped in the 1920s.

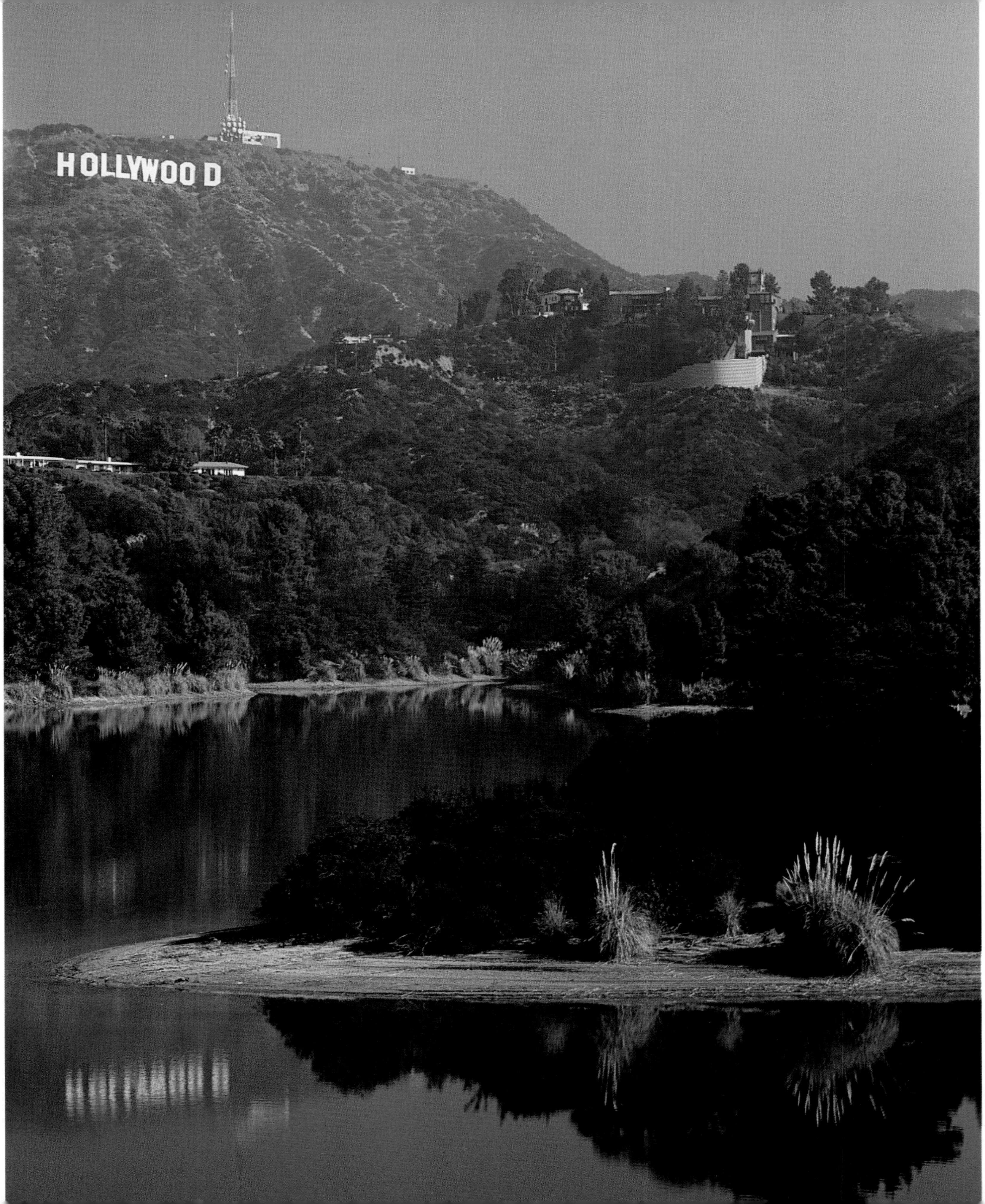
HOLLYWOOD

ABOVE: The library is furnished with antique furniture and prints from Madonna's photography collection. RIGHT: The dining room has an attractively coffered ceiling and a Venetian chandelier. OPPOSITE, CLOCKWISE FROM TOP LEFT: The main bedroom, with its dramatic striped fabric, has French windows that open to one of the house's splendid views. The octagonal bathroom is ingeniously compartmentalized: the shower is straight ahead; hovering above is a fifteen-foot-high cupola edged with decorative stuccowork. Next to the main bedroom, lit by a row of small, high-level windows, is a relaxing sitting room, with striped upholstery fabric that matches the bedroom canopy.

EARLY MODERNISM

FRANK LLOYD WRIGHT ARRIVED IN HOLLYWOOD in 1916, heralding an important new direction for the city's architecture. Busy working on the Imperial Hotel in Tokyo, Wright was invited by theater entrepreneur Aline Barnsdall to design a theater complex and a house on Olive Hill, a substantial piece of land she had purchased in Hollywood. Only the Hollyhock House, as it became known, and two small additional residences were built—not the theater complex—for Barnsdall. But this began Wright's long, though intermittent, association with the city. Wright designed the house to respond to the climate, placing it in a dominant position on its acropolislike site over-looking Hollywood. Just down the street, at the corner of Sunset and Hollywood Boulevards, the Babylonian sets for D. W. Griffith's *Intolerance* had just been built, their ten-story-high bulk visible from Olive Hill. All of this was a far cry from the sedate, bourgeois, family neighborhoods of Oak Park, Illinois, where Wright had lived and worked until 1909.

In 1923 Wright built La Miniatura, widely regarded as one of his finest residences. It was the first of a series of four houses using his experimental textile-block construction, in which cement blocks were knitted together to form a structural entity.

Wright's presence led to the arrival of three other architects in Los Angeles who were to help shape the city. His son, Lloyd Wright, previously a landscape architect, was brought in to help with the Hollyhock House during his father's repeated absences for work on the Imperial Hotel. After finishing this project and assisting with the textile-block houses, Lloyd Wright began his own successful architecture practice.

After a period spent working at Wright's Taliesin, Wisconsin, studio, the young Austrian architect Rudolph Schindler was brought to California by Wright to supervise construction of the Hollyhock House. A former student of Otto Wagner in Vienna, Schindler arrived in the United States in 1913. By the end of 1921 he had set up his own practice in Los Angeles and was building a highly experimental house for himself on King's Road in West Hollywood. This low-cost, wonderfully primitive habitation was a laboratory for Schindler's philosophies of living and design.

During these early years, Schindler wrote to Richard Neutra, a former student acquaintance from Vienna: "I will open my own office in Los Angeles, and in case I get even a little work you can come over and help." Neutra accepted the offer, and, after his own spell working with Wright at Taliesin, he arrived in Los Angeles in 1925.

Schindler's expressionistic designs linked him with Wright's romanticism, whereas Neutra's more rigorous aesthetic reflected his recent exposure to the austerity of European Modernism. For Neutra this proved an enormous advantage. Philip Johnson and Henry Russell Hitchcock, the curators of the 1932 contemporary architecture exhibition at the Museum of Modern Art, excluded anything that did not look European: Neutra's Lovell house was in; Schindler's equally

TOP: Lloyd Wright's 1922 Bollman house, reputed to feature the first use of textile blocks. ABOVE: Schindler's Lovell beach house, 1922–26.

remarkable Lovell beach house, now regarded equally as a masterpiece of early Modernism, was out, consigning him to relative obscurity during his lifetime.

During the 1920s, Art Deco appeared in Los Angeles with a flourish, particularly in the realm of commercial architecture. Zig-Zag Moderne was a popular variant. The opulence associated with this decoratively rich style made it inappropriate for the Depression era of the 1930s, however, and it was replaced by the less extravagant Streamline Moderne.

The age of streamlining affected everything from radios to automobiles, and L.A. became the capital of this evocative style, which became especially popular with the public. "The whole period of Streamline Moderne reflects the mystique about L.A. and its association with the automobile," explains Teresa Grimes of the L.A. Conservancy. Sadly, the best example of all, Pan Pacific Auditorium, was left to decay by the L.A. County authorities and has been demolished.

During the 1930s Schindler and Neutra were joined by a larger, younger group of Modernists, including Gregory Ain, Raphael Soriano, Harwell Harris, and Quincy Jones, who developed together a distinctive southern California style that culminated in the postwar Case Study House Program (1945–60) launched by John Entenza and his magazine *Art and Architecture*.

THE HOLLYHOCK HOUSE

BY FRANK LLOYD WRIGHT

THE SITE CHOSEN BY ALINE BARNSDALL for the Hollyhock House was dramatic: a thirty-six-acre hill that rises to a height of five hundred feet between Hollywood and Sunset Boulevards. This "eminence," as it was known locally, commanded views in all directions and was covered with olive groves.

The period of Hollyhock House's construction was long and tempestuous. Barnsdall's strong-willed spirit matched Wright's, and Wright's commitment to supervise construction of the Imperial Hotel in Tokyo during the same period made things more difficult. His long absences meant that supervision was delegated to his son Lloyd, and subsequently to Rudolph Schindler.

The Hollyhock House sits with battened walls constructed of hollow tile and stucco edged with stylized friezes depicting hollyhocks, Barnsdall's favorite flower. It represented a new direction for Wright's work, inspired by his emotional reaction to southern California. The house is entered via a cramped passageway typical of Wright's designs: the front door is made of reinforced concrete, cleverly shaped to fit the walls, which slope back like a Mayan vault. The interior spaces expand gradually until a loggia is reached, opening onto an internal courtyard on one side and the voluminous living room on the other. The loggia doors fold away, and, with no threshold, the space flows freely between the interior and exterior. This was a new idea in the evolution of Modernist spatial design, possibly inspired by Wright's experiences of screened pavilions in Japan.

The courtyard is flanked on one side by a colonnade and on the other by a glazed gallery, and extends to a semicircular amphitheater and circular pool, above which the two ends of the building are connected by a bridge between Barnsdall's bedroom suite and the guest quarters.

The living room is dominated by a fireplace, surmounted by a carved stone relief that depicts, in abstracted form, the house, its owner, and the site. A skylight placed above and a water-filled moat below contribute to the gathering of all four elements at this spiritual focal point. As the house was to be occupied by just two people—Barnsdall and her daughter—Wright designed furniture with an architectural scale to break up an otherwise daunting space. This exists today in reproduction form.

Barnsdall never really settled in the house. In 1923 she commissioned another house from Wright in Beverly Hills, but this was never built. In 1926 the Hollyhock House was passed on to the city of Los Angeles. It is now looked after by the Cultural Affairs Department and is open to the public.

ABOVE: The living-room wing of Hollyhock House, with balcony and reflecting pool, extends out to the west, embracing an expanse of lawn. OPPOSITE: An upper-level bridge, containing a passage linking the upper-floor family rooms, spans the eastern end of the internal courtyard. A pool is surrounded by curved steps, forming an amphitheater. The frieze extending around the sloping upper walls depicts stylized hollyhocks, Aline Barnsdall's favorite flower.

ABOVE: The table and chairs in the dining room were designed by Wright for the house. The kitchen can be glimpsed through the open door. RIGHT: The windows of a small day-room in the southeast corner of the house are glazed with stained glass, also designed by Wright. OPPOSITE: A colonnade edges the central courtyard. Upper-level walkways link areas of the roof, which was considered an extension of the living space.

ABOVE: The central feature of the house is the cast-concrete living room fireplace, which, with pool and skylight, thematically brings together the four elements. Its carved relief by Lloyd Wright features a stylized depiction of an Indian princess—Aline Barnsdall herself—seated on a throne and gazing out over the desert landscape. The abstracted design is reminiscent of Navajo sand-paintings. BELOW: A Japanese screen from Wright's collection of oriental art and a reproduction Wright chair occupy a corner of the living room. RIGHT: To unify the huge living room while dividing it into areas for different activities, Wright designed large-scale furniture elements. Reproductions of these have now been installed in the living room.

LA MINIATURA

BY FRANK LLOYD WRIGHT

IN 1922, WITH THE HOLLYHOCK HOUSE nearing completion, Wright was approached by Mrs. George Millard to design a small house in Pasadena. Alice Millard was a widow of considerable sophistication; she had inherited her husband's rare book business and loved antique furniture. In 1906, she and her husband had commissioned a classic Prairie house from Wright in Highland Park, Illinois. Here in California she was ready for something new, and a visit to the Hollyhock House made a strong impression. As Wright recalled, "Gradually I unfolded to her the scheme of the textile block–slab house gradually forming in my mind since I got home from Japan. She wasn't frightened by the idea. Not at all."

The site, which they chose together, featured a large flat expanse—a conventionally ideal site for a house—and an adjoining arroyo. Wright chose to place the house straddling the arroyo, giving it a sense of drama and theatricality.

La Miniatura is a house of delicately vertical proportions, a rare departure from the usual pronounced horizontality of Wright's houses, and one of Wright's most romantic visions. Mirrored by a reflecting pool and framed by giant eucalyptus trees, it resembles at first glimpse a temple lost in the jungle.

The cubistic form of the building is dimensionally controlled by the cement blocks' sixteen-inch module, which is imposed as a grid over every surface. This has resulted in a design of purity and simplicity. The house is entered from a door placed in the corner of a small courtyard, positioned between the house and garage and edged by a low wall that overlooks the arroyo below. This entry door opens into a compact, low-ceilinged vestibule set back from the rear corner of the living room, and begins a sequence of beautifully articulated spaces on three levels.

Stepping out from the underside of a balcony that stretches across the entire width of the room, the space soars dramatically to fifteen feet. Rows of French doors open onto a cantilevered balcony overhanging the reflecting pool and the lower arroyo. Light filters into the interior through cruciform slits in the patterned concrete blocks; these perforated surfaces resemble the latticed stone screens found in the Mughal palaces of India.

Mrs. Millard died in 1938, and the house was bought by the grandparents of the current owner, Nicole Daniels. After many years of struggling to maintain the rapidly aging building, Daniels brought in architect Michael Mekeel and artist-designer Annie Kelly to help resolve fundamental problems arising from Wright's unconventional building ideas.

Major structural repairs have been made to the main building and to the linked studio (a later addition by Lloyd Wright). Meanwhile, Kelly developed a stylistic theme for the interiors, uniting the Craftsman style of the period with the building's more exotic aspirations. The living room is anchored by a large eighteenth-century Japanese textile, which is reflected by a framed mirror of similar scale on the opposite side of the room. Japanese Tonsu chests are placed under each to emphasize the repetition. Wired silk hanging lamps, designed by Fortuny, bring out the *piano nobile* quality of the room, a reference to the Italian palazzi beloved by Alice Millard.

The dining room, kitchen, and library are on the lower floor. The dining room extends onto a terrace overlooking the arroyo garden and reflecting pool. Here Wright's hand is less obvious. The walls are of plaster, and only the long redwood windows and harmonious proportions of the rooms link this level with the others in the house. Consequently, Kelly chose colors that are more vibrant; the dining room, for example, has been painted a vivid yellow that glows in the shafts of the late afternoon sun.

Wright stacked a bedroom on each of the three floors. The master bedroom occupies most of the upper level. Using dra-

One of Wright's most romantic visions, La Miniatura resembles a temple lost in the jungle, mirrored by a reflecting pool and framed by giant eucalyptus trees.

matically long brown silk curtains, Kelly framed a view over the upper arroyo like a Japanese landscape. Then she brought in fresco artist Christian Granvelle to unify this tall room with its small upper mezzanine using a coat of dusky pink-tinted plaster.

At the top of the house there is a small door that leads to another spatial surprise. Here, Wright created another kind of space—a high viewing platform over distant roofs to the surrounding hills, backed by a textile-block wall.

While small in scale, La Miniatura seems much larger due to its succession of carefully articulated spaces. There is a certain peace that sits on this house; in the stillness of the afternoon a shaft of sunlight across a patterned block wall gives the illusion of an ancient building recently excavated. La Miniatura has shaped Daniels's sense of aesthetics over the years, and she has maintained the house with the care of a conservator. It is still regarded as one of Wright's most important designs, and was certainly one of his own favorites: "I would rather have built this little house," he wrote, "than St. Peter's in Rome."

ABOVE RIGHT: A mirror in the living room is placed to reflect a similarly framed Oriental textile on the opposite wall. Hanging lanterns are reproductions of Fortuny designs, and the coffee table is by Garouste and Bonetti. RIGHT: A view from the street: the entry courtyard is seen to the left; a garage door is to the right.
OPPOSITE: This end of the living room is anchored by an 18th-century Oriental embroidered textile and a 19th-century Japanese Tonsu chest. Kelly chose furniture inspired by Jean-Michel Frank to harmonize with Wright's geometric architecture. The space is illuminated by glazed doors opening onto a terrace and by cruciform perforations in the textile block, which cast slivers of light across interior surfaces.

RIGHT: Kelly encased an unprepossessing brick fireplace in copper sheeting to reflect light from the windows at the other end of the room and placed a mirror above for the same purpose. Wright might have approved—it was a strategy he often employed himself. BELOW: Framed by yellow silk curtains, the dining room opens onto a terrace and the lower arroyo. The Craftsman chairs are by Charles Limbert and the table was designed by Kathleen Spiegelman. The lamp was made by Gianni Bodo based on Giacometti designs. The dresser is by Stickley. OPPOSITE: The master bedroom enjoys morning light and a view of the upper arroyo. The windows are hung with silk curtains. To the right, a 19th-century Russian fabric hangs above a Craftsman dresser.

ABOVE: A quiet corner off the living room is furnished with a Craftsman chair and desk. The frescoed wall and ceiling treatment is by Christian Granvelle. LEFT: Standing next to a perforated section of wall in a corner of the living room is an 18th-century Chinese Buddha figure. OPPOSITE: The baronial-looking fireplace, with its ornate metalwork and textile-block surrounds.

THE STORER HOUSE

BY FRANK LLOYD WRIGHT

DESIGNED AS AN ORGANIC EXTENSION of its rugged environment, Wright's Storer house—second of the textile-block houses—rises on a series of terraces set into a Hollywood hillside, its cement blocks mixed with decomposed granite from the site itself.

The house faces south, the sunlight filtering into its interior spaces through a lofty colonnaded facade, which is topped by a flat projecting cornice. As with the other textile-block houses, the interior surfaces are of the same concrete as the exterior, adding a cavelike homogeneity to a house that already enjoys an organic intimacy with its site. This continuity of materials also enhances the flow of space between interior rooms and adjacent exterior terraces.

In the absence of a conventional entry door, the house is entered from the main terrace, through one of the openings in the colonnade next to an ornamental lily pond. The low-ceilinged living area inside is balanced by a dining area at one end and a fireplace and comfortable seating at the other. Stairs wrap around and behind the fireplace and flow up to a sunny upper-level living room, at each end of which doors open to terraces with views of the city. The western terrace is reached by another short flight of stairs that similarly rotate around a second fireplace, above the first, to a balcony that looks back into the room.

The bedrooms are set between the two levels, behind the stairs. These are ventilated not by windows, but by perforated blocks, which can be sealed by a sliding screen.

Maintenance has proved to be a thorny problem with Wright's textile-block houses, involving expenses well beyond the reach of the average homeowner. It was especially fortunate, then, that the Storer house was bought in 1984 by movie producer and Wright enthusiast Joel Silver.

He found the house in a sadly deteriorated condition, but instead of renovating it in a conventional way just to keep it "alive," Silver hired a team—led by restoration architect Martin Eli Weil and including Wright's architect grandson Eric Lloyd Wright and interior decorator Linda Marder—and began a complete process of rehabilitation. "Restoring the house," he says, "took a year—about the same length of time it takes to make a movie. They're similar projects. The team work is the same."

ABOVE: The 1923–24 Storer house is built into a steep, terraced slope in the Hollywood hills. OPPOSITE: Wright designed the dining chairs and table; the latter is from the 1908 Isabel Roberts house. The painting is by Frank Myers, and the gilded candelabrum is by Tiffany.

ABOVE: These chairs and table in the upper living room were designed by Lloyd Wright for his Sowden house. RIGHT: The light-filled upper living room is filled with furniture designed by Frank Lloyd Wright, including an adjustable armchair (center) from his 1902 W. E. Martin house. Silver had the standing lamps that frame the view fabricated from previously unrealized Wright designs. A rare Weller Sicard pot stands in the center. Behind it, on the fireplace, is a pot by Teco. The banjo on the stairs is by Bugatti.

THE FREEMAN HOUSE

BY FRANK LLOYD WRIGHT

THE FREEMAN HOUSE WAS THE THIRD of the textile-block houses and was a return to the intimate scale of La Miniatura. Set into a steep hillside overlooking Highland Avenue in Hollywood, the house is entered from the street at living-room level. A narrow passage leads past the kitchen into a large living room, which is designed symmetrically, on axis with a dramatic view over Hollywood. On the floor below are two bedrooms and a projecting terrace, which overhangs the steeply cascading hillside below.

The main volumes of the house, both upper and lower, form a perfect cube, which reinforces the tightly geometric design of the house, with its sixteen-inch-block grid. Windows at each of the front corners cascade continuously from the roof overhang down to the sills of the bedrooms on the floor below.

The Freeman house marked a point where Wright left most of his references to the architectural past and began to embrace Modernism, on his terms. La Miniatura predates it by only a year, but it has a distinct nineteenth-century feel. The Freeman house, especially with its radical mitered windows— their first expression in residential design—firmly embraces the twentieth century.

TOP: The south view of the 1924 Freeman house, a house designed essentially as a perfect cube. ABOVE: A corner of the living room, showing perforated-block wall and the mitered corner window. OPPOSITE: Complemented by a giant euphorbia, the glazing ascends without interruption between the lower and upper floors, and is cleverly integrated with the adjacent blockwork.

THE ENNIS HOUSE

BY FRANK LLOYD WRIGHT

THE SERPENTINE DRIVE UP TO THE Hollywood hilltop site of the Ennis house is punctuated by fleeting views of a Mayan fortress-like presence high above. The road finally wraps around the house, circumnavigating the vast retaining walls of the lower elevations and arriving at the hole-in-the-wall entry. This small door is the only sign of habitation in the blank, battered exterior.

A tour of the house—the last of the textile-block houses built—reveals a theatrically choreographed progression of spaces from compressed to soaring, and from dark to light. The somber, tunnellike entry gates open to a dazzling south-facing terrace, with its dramatic view over the city. From here a cramped, dark entry (suggestive of a medieval keep) and staircase lead up to a lofty, brightly lit loggia and to a sequence of living areas, baronial in scale and mood and evocative of a movie set. They were, in fact, used as a location for the movie *Blade Runner*. The loggia continues through and beyond these areas, creating a hundred-foot-long axis from one end of the house to the other. There are dramatic views to either side of the living areas: a swimming pool and mountains to the north, and a sweeping view of the city, with the ocean beyond, to the south.

LEFT: Resembling a pre-Columbian temple on a mountaintop, the 1924 Ennis house overlooks Hollywood. ABOVE: The baronial living room. Above the fireplace is a mosaic panel. OPPOSITE: A textile-block wall edges the pool and a view of Griffith Park.

THE KING'S ROAD HOUSE

BY RUDOLPH SCHINDLER

IN 1921, RUDOLPH SCHINDLER DECIDED TO BUILD a house for himself and his wife, Pauline; it became the most innovative residential project of its time in both America and Europe.

Following a camping trip to Yosemite, the Schindlers bought a lot on King's Road in West Hollywood, a neighborhood then surrounded by open fields. Irving Gill's Dodge House (destroyed by developers in the 1970s) was one of the few other houses on the street. The embryonic community of Beverly Hills could be glimpsed in the distance, and the ragged profile of the Hollywood hills formed a backdrop to the north. The house was to be shared by another couple, the Chases, who were artists from Chicago.

The Schindlers were by this time socially established in the milieu of artists and free spirits pursuing "modern" ideas of living and creative expression. Prominent among them was an important future client, Dr. Philip Lovell, for whom Schindler was to design the Lovell beach house. Naturopath Lovell was a successful journalist (his "Care of the Body" column was a popular feature in the *Los Angeles Times*) and an enthusiastic promoter of a natural outdoor approach to living. Schindler outlined his concept for his own house in one of Lovell's columns: "Our rooms will descend close to the ground and the garden will become an integral part of the house. The distinction between indoors and outdoors will disappear. . . . It will cease being a group of dens, some larger ones for social effect, and a few smaller ones (bedrooms) in which to herd the family. Each individual will want a private room to gain a background for his life. He will sleep in the open."

Eschewing conventional living arrangements and with an unheard-of nod to sexual equality, Schindler provided a similarly sized studio for each occupant, arranged in a novel pinwheel plan around two open patios, each shared by a couple. The Chases entered from one side of the property, the Schindlers from the other. From each entry, steps led up to separate sleeping porches built onto the roof, which gave vertical punctuation to the low, ground-hugging profile.

There was a shared kitchen—each couple took turns with the cooking arrangements—and a guest room. The patios were equipped with outdoor fireplaces to provide warmth for the frequently held outdoor soirées.

The design of the studios was influenced by the Schindlers' trip to Yosemite. As Schindler wrote: "They fulfill the basic requirements of the camper's shelter: a protected back, an open front, a fireplace, and a roof." Built of concrete, redwood, and canvas, the house evoked the sensation of living in a tent and communing with nature. Sliding screens, which were removed entirely during warm weather, opened onto the patio. With the concrete-slab floor at the same level as the patio, there was a direct flow of space between interior and exterior areas.

This was a direct exploration of the ideas of indoor and outdoor space pioneered by Wright in the Hollyhock House. As historian Kathryn Smith noted, "He considered the entire lot, 100 by 200 feet, as a living space and then divided it into enclosed and open zones." Schindler even planted privet hedges to visually extend the wall planes into the landscape.

The concrete walls were poured in sections on the site and tilted up into position, a technique pioneered by Irving Gill. Between each section was a narrow slot of glass. The sloping walls and ground-hugging profile of the building strongly suggested indigenous adobe structures, which Schindler had visited on a trip through the Southwest in 1915. Its silhouette in early photographs blends beautifully with the empty terrain surrounding it.

The larger of two courtyards serves as an outdoor room for two of the three studios. There is an outdoor fireplace in the wall to the left; a covered sleeping platform can be seen on the roof.

Schindler's innovations were sometimes wildly impractical, however well they fit the nature-loving spirit of the times. Other houses with sleeping porches had bedrooms that could be used in inclement conditions. But the occupants at King's Road were forced to wrap themselves in tarpaulins to stay dry when the rains fell. And at a time when central heating was standard in every house regardless of size, the Schindler residence offered only the fireplace as a source of heat—and the rooms were poorly insulated.

For most of the year, however, the occupants enjoyed the experience of living close to the earth and to nature. Schindler's innovative and sociological strategies were well ahead of their time and were to define California living for succeeding generations.

ABOVE: The entry, with one of the giant stands of bamboo that are a feature of the landscaping. RIGHT: The floors of the studio are level with the courtyard, and with the screens pulled back there is minimal division between inside and outside. The furniture is by Schindler.

THE LOVELL HOUSE

BY RICHARD NEUTRA

THE LOVELL HOUSE INTRODUCED the machine aesthetic of International Modernism to the United States. Neutra's first house, it is one of only two American houses recognized as early monuments of the International style; the other is Schindler's Lovell beach house. Both houses were built for the same clients: Philip and Leah Lovell.

The Neutra commission, received while he was working and living *en famille* with Schindler, caused a rift in a long, supportive, and important friendship. Neutra had only recently arrived in Los Angeles, and he managed to secure the commission by giving the false impression that Schindler was to oversee the design. Schindler must have ultimately felt satisfaction, though, knowing that the Lovells found the house too formal and stiff and chose instead to live in the beach house.

Overlooking a verdant valley and the city beyond, the Lovell house is built into a steep hillside, but its lightness of form is such that the asymmetrical cantilevered layers seem to levitate up from each other. Today this is visible only in old photographs; foliage now hides most of the front elevation.

The house is entered via a raised walkway at the upper level. A dramatic staircase wrapped by a vast window wall leads from the entry lobby down into a long, airy living room. A single door at one end opens onto a paved patio and lawn (Neutra's mastery of indoor-outdoor relationships was to come later). The rest of the house is spatially conventional: a dining area is tucked around a corner at the far end of the living

room, and bedrooms on the upper level are small, with attached sleeping porches, some now glazed in.

Neutra loved catalog-bought fixtures. He believed in standardization and mass production, and the Model T Ford headlights that illuminate the staircase represent ideals he shared with Henry Ford.

TOP: The living room of the 1929 Lovell house, with furniture by the architect. ABOVE: Visitors arrive at the upper-level entry. A staircase leads down a floor to the living room. The cascading garden elevation of the house is now obscured by foliage. OPPOSITE: The staircase, seen from the living room. The light fixture Neutra chose to set into the stair wall—a head lamp from a Model T Ford—symbolized his love of mass production.

THE SAMUELS-NOVARRO HOUSE

BY LLOYD WRIGHT
INTERIOR RENOVATION BY SCHWEITZER/BIM

LLOYD WRIGHT'S SAMUELS-NOVARRO HOUSE was built in 1926 for writer Luis Samuels, then sold to silent-movie actor Ramon Novarro. With a richly patinated copper-clad facade fashioned with arrowhead motifs, the house rises dramatically from a winding street in the Hollywood hills. Designed the year after the 1925 *Exposition Internationale des Arts Décoratifs et Industriels Modernes* in Paris, its facade resembles a vast piece of Art Deco costume jewelry.

The house is set into a narrow, precipitous hillside lot sandwiched between streets above and below. Pergolas extend along terraces cut into the slope. The front entry is from the street above, while the garage is on the street below.

When actress Diane Keaton bought the house in 1989, little more than the exterior shell remained in its original condition. The spatially constricted interiors had been much altered by a succession of owners in the 1950s and '60s and were in need of creative reinterpretation.

Architect Josh Schweitzer of Schweitzer/BIM stripped the interior down to its bare bones, removed nonstructural partitions, made new openings in structural walls, and revealed the concrete floors, which were then treated and colored to add warmth and patina. Existing aluminum sliding doors and windows were discarded and new ones were made to Wright's original designs. No detail was overlooked: even the original faucets were sandblasted and sealed.

As little of Wright existed on the inside except the space itself, it became apparent that new interior architecture must be created to match the power of the exterior. "The house kept changing from the moment Wright designed it," says Schweitzer. "I thought the most important thing was to understand his sense of space. It was a small house, but by making things tall and narrow, he gave it grandeur."

Schweitzer's predilection for chunky shapes and unexpected scale relationships influenced design decisions throughout the house. Inside the entry hall, visitors are confronted by a giant clock set into the stairs. An oversize lamp and a massive cubistic entertainment cabinet animate the living areas. Here and elsewhere, ceilings are lowered in places to conceal lighting and air-conditioning, increasing the spatial dynamic. Another boldly scaled cabinet and jumbo lamp lend order to the studio space on the floor below. Even handrails have a massive four-inch-square section.

Schweitzer succeeded in creating interior spaces as dramatic as the exteriors. His sculpted forms give importance and livability to previously drab and cramped interiors. Surprisingly, his overscale elements, which might be expected to have made the interiors seem smaller, have the opposite effect.

ABOVE: With a richly patinated copper-clad facade fashioned with arrowhead motifs, the 1926 Samuels-Novarro house rises dramatically from a winding street in the Hollywood hills. OPPOSITE: The arrowhead motif even appears underwater. The French doors open to the living room; the main bedroom is overhead.

LEFT: Schweitzer's overscale design elements are apparent throughout the house. Visitors are greeted by an overscale clock in the entry, while the stair balustrade is four inches square in sections. BOTTOM LEFT: Stripping the lower floor to the bare bones, Schweitzer created a workable study space, again featuring overscale elements, such as a massive floor lamp. BELOW: Attention is lavished on the smallest details: the brass faucets were sandblasted to get the right textural effect. BOTTOM RIGHT: Schweitzer used Wright's arrowhead motif to focus attention on the living room fireplace. OPPOSITE: The sitting room, looking toward the pool. The chair and sofa are by Paul Laszlo.

CARPENTER · EARLY CEMETERIES OF THE CITY OF LOS ANGELES

THE DOLORES DEL RIO HOUSE

BY CEDRIC GIBBONS AND DOUGLAS HONNOLD

PERHAPS THE MOST GLAMOROUS of all the movie-star houses built during the golden age of Hollywood was the sleek Moderne-style home created in 1929 by art director Cedric Gibbons (with the help of architect Douglas Honnold) as a showcase for his bride, the Mexican actress Dolores del Rio.

They were a glamorous couple. Gibbons ran the legendary MGM art department from 1924 until 1958. He designed the Oscar statuette, and then won a total of twelve of them for the set designs of such films as *Pride and Prejudice, Gaslight, Little Women, An American in Paris,* and *Julius Caesar.* He was tall, attractive, and stylish, sporting a Ronald Colman pencil mustache. His wife was one of the most exotic and successful of the silent movie stars, traveling around town in an immense Cadillac Eight Custom town car with a chauffeur *and* a footman to open and close the doors.

Viewed from its quiet Santa Monica Canyon cul-de-sac, the house presents an inscrutable facade. The interior, however, resembles a 1930s Deco movie set. The visitor steps into a lavish salon with shiny black linoleum floors, enormous banquettes, and a staircase with a lustrous aluminum balustrade, down which Del Rio made an entrance once her guests had assembled.

The staircase leads up to a large, airy living room with views over the canyon. One notices, appropriately in a house designed for a movie star, an abundance of mirrors, most evident in Del Rio's spectacular dressing room and bathroom.

ABOVE: The partially paved garden terrace at the rear of the house. The upper living room window is in the center of this view. Stepping stones in the foreground lead to the tennis court. The pool is to the left of the photo. OPPOSITE: Viewed from the street, the house presents a sleekly inscrutable Moderne-style facade, with the stepback of the door echoed at the roofline.

PRECEDING PAGES: The International Style garden elevation, with its crisp fenestration and flat roofs, is a backdrop for high-style outdoor entertaining. ABOVE: The upstairs living room features comfortable 1930s leather armchairs and a polished black linoleum floor. Moderne-style stepped stucco work—seen here on the ceiling and in the doorway—appears throughout the house.

LEFT: The living room fireplace is a tour de force of Moderne styling. BELOW: The stylish tennis pavilion, walls and ceiling paneled with linoleum and copper strips and featuring a curvaceous copper balustrade, resembles a 1930s nightclub. Furniture was chosen by designer Barbara Barry. Steps lead up to the garden.

POST-1930s REVIVALISM

DURING THE 1930S, REVIVALISM CONTINUED UNABATED, with Spanish Colonialism yielding to new fashions: American Colonial, Regency, Monterey, and English Tudor among them. Although the Depression hit southern California as it did elsewhere, the wealthy were less affected than the man in the street, and designers of luxury houses in Los Angeles were still able to enjoy successful careers. The most sophisticated group of revivalists in America—including Wallace Neff, Roland Coate, John Woolf, James Dolena, Paul Williams, and John Byers—worked in Los Angeles during this period, which was highlighted by the evolution of the Hollywood Regency style, developed further in the 1940s by John Woolf.

Woolf, an architect as well as an interior designer, set up his practice in Los Angeles toward the end of the 1930s, wooing a celebrity clientele with his innovative designs. The commission that established his career was a Beverly Hills pied-à-terre for New York decorator James Pendleton. The stylishly mannered Pendleton House was modeled on drawings of pavilions in Versailles, shown to the architect by Elsie de Wolfe.

"The Hollywood Regency style was theatrical," comments John Chase in his book *Exterior Decoration*, "and resembled a stage set. This architecture of glamor required the seemingly effortless balancing between the formal and the casual, as well as the knack for well placed exaggeration and well chosen omission . . . it was the perfect architecture to represent the Hollywood that had brought 'a world of silken underwear, exotic surroundings, and moral plasticity' to the United States through the medium of film."

This style, taken up by both architects and decorators, was a sophisticated distillation of English Regency (the symmetrical pavilion facades of Sir John Soane were a particular influence), and American Colonial, which favored low-pitched roofs and simple boxy forms.

The abstracted use of blank walls played against carefully zoned areas of detail—which featured in the designs of George Washington Smith and Wallace Neff—was also an influence. The final flourish came with a touch of French chic: Mansard roofs and faux pavilions *à la* Versailles.

The architect Cliff May began his long and prolific career in the 1920s as a Spanish Colonial Revivalist in San Diego (he was descended from one of the early Spanish land-grant families). In 1932, he moved to Los Angeles, and during that decade evolved the familiar ranch house design that was to make him famous. However, his 1940 Provençal-style Blow house was a conspicuous deviation from his usual vocabulary.

During the 1920s the designs of Revivalists in southern California received wide attention from the critics and the press. This potent form of encouragement dwindled during the 1930s as the focus of attention shifted

TOP: The Sol Wurtzel house, 1932, one of Wallace Neff's grander essays in the Italian style. ABOVE: The elegant rear terrace of a 1960s pavilion-style house by James Dolena.

to Modernism, and after the war it was reduced to almost nil. Not surprisingly, this was discouraging for architects such as Neff, whose career extended until 1970.

In recent years, on the east coast at least, Revivalist house design, riding on the coattails of post-Modernism, has again received critical consideration as a "style" alternative to the much-denigrated Modernism. Such architects as Robert A. M. Stern and Allan Greenberg have been producing remarkably sensitive Revivalist houses. In southern California, however, the Neffs, the Smiths, the Woolfs, the Williamses, and the Coates are missed. So too are the earlier generations of architect-builders who gave us countless well-mannered Mediterranean revival houses. Sadly, no one worthy of note has replaced them. Opportunities for continuing a great regional tradition have been lost: the multitude of period-style houses built in Los Angeles in the 1970s and '80s have been invariably overscale, badly detailed, and poorly proportioned. They have proliferated like a disease through the hitherto gracious, attractively scaled neighborhoods of Beverly Hills, Brentwood, and Pacific Palisades.

THE PALEY HOUSE

BY PAUL WILLIAMS

PAUL WILLIAMS, WITH A LONG CAREER spanning from 1922 to 1973, was one of the city's more successful and prolific architects. He was perhaps best known for two of its most stylish and elegant postwar landmarks: the 1950s additions to the Beverly Hills Hotel, and the futuristic '60s theme building at Los Angeles International Airport. He also designed a number of distinctive houses for film industry personalities, including Lon Chaney, Frank Sinatra, Lucille Ball and Desi Arnaz, Tyrone Power, and Anthony Quinn. In 1936 Paul Williams designed one of his best houses, for Columbia Broadcasting System president Jay Paley, on a wedge-shaped site in Holmby Hills.

A gently curving driveway leads to a decoratively paved forecourt and the delicately detailed facade of the Georgian Colonial-style house. An axis, popular with many Los Angeles estates in the 1930s and '40s, traverses the forecourt, passes through the house, and extends out to the pool, ending with the pool pavilion.

ABOVE: The curves in the swimming pool are seemingly generated by undulations in the water. OPPOSITE: The Paley forecourt is paved in a design radiating from a central zodiac-patterned brass plaque—echoed by the swimming pool's motif—and leads to the delicately detailed facade of the Georgian Colonial-style house.

ABOVE AND BELOW: Williams gave the pool pavilion and the back of the house a Regency twist, linking both buildings by using the attenuated columns that were a distinctive feature of this style. RIGHT: The swimming pool, one of the most beautiful in southern California, adds an Art Deco flourish. The tiles, imported from France, form a spectacular double sunburst motif, interspersed by the twelve signs of the zodiac.

THE PENDLETON HOUSE

BY JOHN WOOLF

THE PENDLETON HOUSE REPRESENTS one of the first, as well as one of the most successful, manifestations of the Hollywood Regency style. Perhaps John Woolf's best house, it was a social as well as an architectural success. Artist and designer Tony Duquette remembers a typical Sunday lunch in the pool pavilion, "with Garbo calling from the pool that we mustn't look, because as usual she refused to wear a costume!" The front facade has all the attributes of this architecture of stylistic extremes. Its symmetrical surface is blank and mannered, punctuated by an oval niche on either side of the attenuated entrance flanked by exterior curtains and topped by a mansard roof.

The plan is also symmetrical, with an axis beginning at the oval entry door and terminating at the pool pavilion. The hall opens into the living room, its famous fireplace surmounted by a plate-glass window (the flue is set to one side). The view through this window is of another fireplace in the distant pool pavilion, which has been used by the current owner, producer Robert Evans, as a screening room since he bought and redecorated the property in the 1970s.

To one side of the pool is a formal topiary garden, while a two-hundred-year-old sycamore overshadows the lawn opposite, sheltering an outdoor dining area.

Although the estate is not large, the disposition of its elements is particularly well thought out. The interplay of architecture and landscaping makes full use of every inch of the available space.

ABOVE: The 1940 Pendleton house did much to establish John Woolf's career. Perhaps the most successful manifestation of the popular Hollywood Regency style, it incorporates features borrowed from French architecture, including the Mansard roof, which became a hallmark of the style. OPPOSITE: The flamboyant entry door is flanked by curtains and a pair of oval niches.

OPPOSITE: Where the chimney ought to be in the living room fireplace is a window with a view of a similar chimney, in the pool pavilion at the end of the garden.
ABOVE LEFT: A dining room window offers a glimpse of a small pool and fountain, surrounded by lush plantings, that projects into the garden. The swimming pool is beyond.
ABOVE RIGHT: The oval niches of the pool pavilion match those of the entrance to the house. LEFT: Between the house and the pool pavilion is a large, oval pool.

THE FREDERICK BLOW HOUSE

BY CLIFF MAY

THE FREDERICK BLOW HOUSE WAS BUILT IN 1940 for a wealthy businessman anxious to cure his French wife of homesickness. Designed to evoke memories of Provençal farmhouses, it was a success.

The house, surrounded by pines and three acres of landscaped gardens, is set on a ridge high above Brentwood, overlooking the ocean. It is perhaps the only late-period Cliff May house to deviate from his California ranch style. May, whose extensive library included several important volumes on stone cutting, hired craftsmen from the Forest Lawn Memorial Park to do the stonework, which is of a high standard (especially the cantilevered stone steps that rotate upward from the circular entry hall).

The present owners, Nancy and Zubin Mehta, bought the house from actor Steve McQueen and actress-dancer Neile Adams in 1974 and restored it, adding elements that have enriched its European ambience and charm. The wooden entry doors (which were a perfect fit) were found in Milan by Nancy Mehta, who has also filled the house with antiques from France and Italy.

TOP: The stairwell has a rustic, French-country charm. ABOVE: With lofty pine trees and no other house visible from the property, the Provençal-style Blow house successfully evokes the South of France. OPPOSITE: The staircase, with carefully detailed cantilevered stone treads, rises from the circular entry hall.

MID-CENTURY MODERNISM

WHEN WORLD WAR II ENDED, A GOLDEN AGE dawned in suburbia. In sharp contrast to the privations being experienced in Europe, southern California enjoyed an unprecedented period of growth and industrialization. Freeways were built to accommodate the newly colorful, glossy automobiles. Ranch houses appeared by the thousands in brand-new subdivisions, which swallowed up countless acres of orange groves as the boundaries of greater Los Angeles expanded to distant horizons.

Perceiving a failure by architects to address the design challenges offered by the new opportunities in mass housing, John Entenza, the editor of the locally published *Arts and Architecture* magazine, launched his famous Case Study House Program in 1945 to encourage modern designers to produce attractive and cheap housing that employed the latest building technologies. As Esther McCoy put it, "Wright was dandy, but the true path was through standardization."

Thirty-six projects were produced for this program, by architects Craig Ellwood, Eero Saarinen, Charles and Ray Eames, Richard Neutra, and others. All promoted advanced free-flowing plans and new technologies appropriate for mass production. Most were built, and the program attracted wide interest in modern design, establishing Los Angeles as the focus of the nation's Modern movement.

The Case Study houses that were open to the public received more than 360,000 visitors. The houses were in a distinctive style appropriate to the region's friendly climate: they were lightly framed and as transparent as possible. Furniture by Eames, Marcel Breuer, and others added a colorful and often whimsical counterpoint to the abstract characteristics of the architecture. Other architects working at the time, Richard Banta in particular, added to the vocabulary of L.A.'s light-frame Modernism (highlighted in the Case Study program).

Unfortunately, neither the established architects from the prewar era—such as Neutra, Schindler, Soriano, Ain, and H. Harwell Harris—nor the younger Case Study architects managed to connect satisfactorily with the developers who were covering the outlying reaches of the L.A. basin with an unprecedented volume of mass housing.

A significant figure to emerge during the immediate postwar period was John Lautner, a student of Frank Lloyd Wright and the only one of his disciples to establish himself as a major architectural figure. Like Wright before him, Lautner was unimpressed by the work of most of his contemporaries, and particularly not by what he perceived as fashions in architecture. During the 1950s, when he, together with Douglas Honnold and others, helped invent L.A.'s famous "Googie" coffee shop style, Lautner was at the cutting edge of contemporary L.A. architecture. In the 1960s he discovered concrete, which thenceforth became his favorite building material, sparking an evolution of organic house design that has lasted for more than three decades.

The remarkable houses produced during this period have eloquently addressed concerns that, while important to Wright, were barely addressed by the rest of the profession. Lautner has given his clients an elemental experience of comfort, shelter, and space.

Set into the hill below by the W.C. Fields estate is Richard Banta's 1961 Banta house—renovated by Barry Sloane—with Banta's signature folded roof.

His spaces both nurture and shelter with a cavelike enfolding, an experience accompanied by a corresponding point of release: an upthrust of roof revealing the big view of city and ocean. Lautner disagrees with architecture designed from the facade in. "I've never done a facade in my life," he declares. "My architecture works from the inside. The main idea is the internal space, and the ideal internal space has a disappearing, timeless feeling."

In a city noted for pioneering the concept of "indoor-outdoor" architecture, Lautner is the only architect in the past thirty years to have given substantial thought to ways of experiencing the elements, often with extraordinary results. Lautner has enjoyed scant attention in the architectural press during his long career, however. The issues he addresses have been either unfashionable (the press was instead enraptured with the skin-deep charms of post-Modernism) or simply beyond the vocabulary of conventional architectural criticism.

There is, however, another problem: Lautner's architecture, more than most, needs to be experienced in three dimensions.

Rendering it photographically is difficult. The familiar one-point-perspective architectural photograph of a rectilinear space establishes scale. Lautner's spatially complex living areas, which are wonderful in reality, tend to photograph—in unsympathetic hands—like hotel lobbies.

THE EAMES HOUSE

BY CHARLES EAMES

WITH ITS REFRESHING IMPRESSION OF INFORMALITY, the 1949 Eames house is one of the most endearing of Modernist houses. Designed by architect Charles Eames, with the collaboration of Eero Saarinen in its early stages, it was created as part of the Case Study House Program.

Unlike most Modernist masterpieces, the house does not present itself as a formal architectural statement. Deferring to the landscape in its placement, and screened by its extra "facade" of foliage, it is designed to be an incident in its environment, not the main focus. Resembling an overscale child's construction kit, this most relaxed and unserious of houses fulfills its designers' intentions lightly: to provide an unpretentious and playful background for its owners' diverse activities.

The interiors are enlivened by light and shadows from the eucalyptus which penetrate the interior through a variety of translucent and transparent glazed panels. The house is filled with the Eameses' ethnic and folk art collections.

TOP RIGHT: The west end of the Eames house. To the left is a covered patio adjoining the living room; a longitudinal pathway, paved with redwood, is on the right. CENTER RIGHT: Behind the balcony is the bedroom. The hallway leads through first to the entry and then to the kitchen. RIGHT: One of the most memorable features of the Eames house is the vivid coloration of the facade. Ray Eames chose the bright colors to punch through the teasing veil of eucalyptus when viewed, as here, from across the meadow. OPPOSITE: Ray Eames's distinctive use of color is evident in this view of the entry. The stairs can be glimpsed inside the door.

THE LORING HOUSE

BY RICHARD NEUTRA

THE LORING HOUSE IN THE HOLLYWOOD HILLS is a typical Neutra "boxcar" design from the 1950s, so called because of its extruded horizontal shape and fenestration. It has been carefully and stylishly renovated by architects Donna Robertson and Robert McNulty for the current owner.

With a south-facing orientation toward a rectangular pool and a green lawn stretching toward a distant city view, it offers a convincing version of the idyllic L.A. lifestyle. Protected by a broad roof overhang, the oversize glass doors slide away and give the owner the maximum opportunity to enjoy year-round outdoor living.

ABOVE: With the greatest simplicity, the Loring house offers the dream late-1950s L.A. lifestyle: maximum exposure to the sun, a view of the city, a terrace, and a pool. When the broad sliding panels (which Neutra favored in his late career) are pulled back, the interiors—with carpets to match the exterior paving—and exterior merge into a single living area. Neutra designed the poolside chaises. OPPOSITE: At the southeast corner the wall is recessed to allow a glazed return to the bedroom window. The spider-leg column frames a view of the pool.

ABOVE: In the living room, a painting by Gerhard Richter hangs above a slate and oak shelf to the left of a classic Neutra fireplace. The "surfboard" coffee table is by Charles Eames. RIGHT: Neutra offset the small dimensions of the bathroom by designing windows that embrace the view. OPPOSITE: A sliding panel opens the bedroom to the terrace. A chair by Pierre Jeanneret is placed in front of a secondary view of the garden.

THE SINGLETON HOUSE

BY RICHARD NEUTRA
LANDSCAPE DESIGN BY ISAMU NOGUCHI

NOW RESTORED TO ITS ORIGINAL CONDITION, the Singleton house occupies a lofty site above Mulholland Drive near Beverly Glen, with an overview of the Stone Canyon Reservoir. Built in 1959, it typifies Neutra's later design approach. The "machine in the garden" aesthetic of his prewar houses, with their doctrinaire International-style gray-and-white palette, had become less machinelike and responded more sympathetically with the landscape. The Singleton house embraces its surroundings with projecting "spider leg" columns and a reflecting pool, while its interiors are enriched with natural materials: wood, stone, and brick.

A series of steps passes through a rock garden landscaped by the sculptor Isamu Noguchi to arrive below a de Stijl–inspired pergola and the entry door. This leads into a vestibule, which shares space with the living and dining areas. The living room—with its crisp, typically Neutra fireplace—opens onto a garden edged by large trees framing a view of the reservoir, and a large glass panel slides away to remove any barrier between the indoors and the world outside. Next to this, the two glazed planes of the living room intersect at a mitered-glass corner. The structural (spider leg) support extends out beyond the confines of the house and helps frame the view seen from within, a view reflected in the pool below. This corner is the architectural focus of the house and its most memorable feature. Here Neutra achieved far more by sleight of hand than a more grand statement would have done, adding magic and complexity to an otherwise simple house.

TOP: In front of the fireplace is a table by George Nelson. ABOVE: In this view, the dining room is to the left of the living room; beyond the reflecting pool to the right is the master bedroom. OPPOSITE: The living room boasts a view of the reflecting pool and the distant Stone Canyon Reservoir. Rocks placed in the landscaping—seen here next to the Neutra-designed chaises—were the work of Isamu Noguchi.

THE GOLDSTEIN HOUSE

BY JOHN LAUTNER

THE GOLDSTEIN HOUSE IS A REMODELED VERSION of the Sheats residence, which Lautner designed in 1963. In the nineteen years since real estate entrepreneur Jim Goldstein bought the house, built on a steep hillside overlooking Beverly Hills, he has engaged in a continuous collaboration with the architect, remodeling and refining the house to—as he puts it—"museum standards." Goldstein's goal is a perfect 1990s version of a classic 1960s house. Walls have been removed, and a new master suite of concrete and glass has been added. In an obsessive drive for transparency, every steel mullion has been replaced with all-glass detailing. Future plans include a new deck on the south side, next to the dining area and guest rooms, cantilevered out over the view.

From its point of entry, the house offers a carefully modulated sequence of spacial experiences and vistas—a Lautner signature. A narrow entry passage is sheltered by the low extended roof of the house. Rounding a turn, the passage becomes less restricted, fanning out horizontally to an entry courtyard filled with the sound of rushing water. On the left is a long cascade, which actually continues through the glass and into the living room. Stepping stones follow the line of the cascade, leading the eye to the interior.

Passing under the low soffit that edges the courtyard and living room, there is a dramatic transition from a horizontal to a vertical space. A massive but seemingly floating, triangulated cast-concrete roof rises up from the hill's edge on the right, then folds back down to meet the upslope of the hill to

the left of the house. The view ahead through this cavelike living space is partially terminated by a protective downslope of the roof (which reinforces a sense of enclosure), but then is revealed as the roof soars upward. Beyond is a terrace with a pool, which terminates abruptly in a V-shaped parapet, thrusting out into space like the bow of some futuristic liner.

The remodeled open-plan master suite is hidden below the terrace and replaces a series of smaller rooms. A new concrete wall/divider separates the dressing area from the bedroom. Windows set into the back wall of the dressing area reveal glimpses underwater into the swimming pool. Lautner moved the bathroom from a corner to the front edge to provide a view. When Goldstein requested that the washbasin be placed in the outer wall, facing the new view, Lautner obliged with an all-glass basin incorporated into the glass wall; water gushes from a sensor-activated channel. He also installed indoor and outdoor showers (Lautner often designs bathrooms that allow the owners to embrace the elements). A final flourish: at the touch of a button, a section of the deck outside slides away to reveal a Jacuzzi.

ABOVE: In the newly remodeled bathroom, the washbasin is a tour de force, achieving transparency in every detail. Water spouts from a sensor-activated channel (no faucets necessary), is retained by a glass stopper, and drains through another transparent channel. OPPOSITE: The living room looks onto the pool terrace and a view of the city. With the recent remodeling, all the window mullions have been removed, and the glazing is now frameless.

ABOVE: The entry courtyard, with the entry door to the right. Stepping stones lead the eye to the living room. BELOW: This is the view back from the living room to the entry court, with the dining area to the left. RIGHT: The living room is sheltered by the original triangulated concrete canopy and looks over the pool terrace.

TWO POSTWAR DECORATORS

THE YEARS IMMEDIATELY BEFORE AND AFTER World War II were a glamorous period for Los Angeles. The city became a mecca for writers, architects, artists, composers, socialites, intellectuals, and aristocrats fleeing the Nazi threat overshadowing Europe. Artist and decorator Tony Duquette remembers this era as a kind of golden age for Beverly Hills. "Once they had arrived in the States, where did they want to go? Not to New York or Washington—they all flocked to Los Angeles to be with the movie stars!" Remembering the weekly salons at the home of his mentor, Elsie de Wolfe, he comments, "Everyone who had ever been photographed by Beaton or Hoyningen-Huene was there, and it was marvelous."

No one, however, was more glamorous than Elsie de Wolfe, also known by her married name, Lady Mendl. Arriving back in her native New York from war-torn France, the legendary decorator was quickly lured to Hollywood. She set up court in Beverly Hills and transformed its "ugliest house" into a chic salon, and her events soon became as celebrated as those given at her beloved Villa Trianon in Versailles (to which she returned when the war was over).

During the 1930s, the decorator of note was William Haines. From the 1940s onward, he shared the spotlight with Tony Duquette. Duquette, then in his early twenties, was a de Wolfe discovery; she had spotted his elaborate centerpiece at a dinner party in the Pendleton house and immediately hired him to create furniture and *objets*. Swept under her wing, he was pronounced a "genius," and his career was launched.

Duquette, who at the time was essentially an artist, became a decorator, and he worked extensively for the resident film community and for international society abroad. His clients included Elizabeth Arden, Merle Oberon, David Selznick, Jennifer Jones, Mary Pickford, Irene Dunne, J. Paul Getty, and Doris Duke. One of his early commissions, arranged for him by Haines, was the decoration of the Mocambo nightclub on the Sunset Strip. Duquette approached decorating as an artist and it was not unusual for him to integrate found objects or natural elements such as shells in his designs. He soon extended his range to design sets and costumes for movies, ballets, operas, and theater, including the original production of *Camelot,* for which he won a Tony Award.

Like Duquette, William Haines was a decorator to the stars. A top MGM actor himself in the 1920s, Haines made a smooth transition to the world of decorating in the early 1930s. With his movie star contacts and sparkling personality, Haines entered the L.A. decorating scene at the top and remained there throughout his career. Haines's early style was Classical. "I loathe cozy cottages," he once said. "They were made for farmers and peasants, not ladies and gentlemen." He introduced French and English antiques—a welcome antidote to the often gloomy Spanish colonial interiors of the previous decade. He

TOP AND ABOVE: Two views of the living room of the James and Beverly Coburn residence in Beverly Hills, decorated in 1969 by Tony Duquette. The roof beams are covered in appliquéd mother-of-pearl.

then began to add touches of chinoiserie—which he particularly loved—and Regency, as well as an endless stream of innovative ideas of his own.

His office on Sunset Boulevard, now Le Dome restaurant, was a flamboyant showcase for his designs. During his prewar period, Haines did houses for a stream of Hollywood clients, including Leila Hyams and Phil Berg, Jack Warner (whose house was recently bought by David Geffen and is being redecorated by Rose Tarlow), Carole Lombard, William Powell, Norma Shearer, William Goetz, Joan Crawford, and George Cukor. For the latter he teamed with architect James Dolena—who had just designed a series of houses with interiors by the brilliant New York–based Englishman Robsjohn Gibbings—whose witty, part Regency–part neoclassical designs influenced Haines.

After World War II, Haines opened a new office in Beverly Hills, and Ted Graber became a partner. In postwar years, Haines quickly developed a new, more modern style. His last projects were for Ambassador Walter Annenberg: the decoration of his desert home in Palm Springs and, in 1970, the interiors for his ambassadorial residence in Regent's Park, London.

JEAN HOWARD RESIDENCE

BY WILLIAM HAINES

UP A BUSY CANYON ROAD AND HIDDEN by a high wall is the discreet entrance to the house author-photographer Jean Howard moved into with her late husband, the legendary agent and producer Charles Feldman, in 1942.

Howard began her career as a Ziegfeld girl, then was lured west by the promise of Hollywood. She soon married and hosted parties for her husband's clients, who were the most stellar names of the period. She documented her extraordinary life with a camera, both privately and professionally, and published two books: *Jean Howard's Hollywood* and *Travels with Cole Porter.*

Distinguished by a spacious and elegant forecourt, the single-story house has two wings, public and private, separated by a central entry hall. It was decorated in 1942 by Billy Haines with such success that Howard has changed little since. In fact, the walls have never been repainted. It remains, more than fifty years later, a showcase of timeless design.

The powder room, to the right of the entry, was painted by artist Beegle Duquette in the style of Marie Laurencin, the French artist known for her delicate pastels. The hall opens into a bright garden room with leaf green walls. The piano is topped with photographs of some of the personalities who sang and played and visited there, a list that includes Judy Garland, Richard Burton, Frank Sinatra, Cole Porter, Rosalind Russell, and John F. Kennedy.

A central pair of double doors, added by decorator John Woolf, open into a sumptuous mirror-paneled living room,

hung with a gilded eighteenth-century chinoiserie chandelier. Long couches line the walls at each end, strewn with silk cushions which, with their many colors, provide a foil for the green walls. In the center of the room, defining the space, is a round table in front of a carved-wood fireplace. The different seating areas are skillfully designed to accommodate large groups without interrupting the flow of the room.

To be able to entertain well, a room should have the ability to transport its guests out of the everyday world. Furnished with Haines's trademark touches of chinoiserie, Howard's dining room is a formal space that, when lit by candles, becomes magical.

With long hallways, which Tony Duquette enlivened with Moroccan-style lattice screens, the private wing of the house is quietly luxurious. It has hand-painted bathrooms and photos of Howard dressed by Mainbocher.

Many houses today emphasize size over good design. Here is an example of how a well-considered layout and good materials render pointless many of the sprawling temples of bad taste that have sprouted all over the city.

ABOVE: The piano is lined with framed mementos: Cole Porter, Noël Coward, the Oliviers, the Coopers, and, in the foreground, Jean Howard with Norma Shearer and Marty Arrouge.

ABOVE: The lavishly decorated living room is embellished with Haines's signature touches of chinoiserie; note the chandelier and various lamps. LEFT: Modigliani's "Portrait of Elvira" anchors the mirrored wall of the living room.

ABOVE: The dining room is a formal space that becomes magical when lit by candles. The New York decorators Denning and Fourcade replaced the curtains twenty-five years ago, adding even more reds to this richly colored and glamorous room. RIGHT: The detail of a place setting is a reminder of largely bygone times. OPPOSITE: The powder room was decorated in a romantic style by artist Beegle Duquette.

DAWNRIDGE

BY TONY DUQUETTE

THE PINK-TRELLISED FACADE OF DAWNRIDGE, home of artist-decorator Tony Duquette and his artist wife, Beegle, stands above a tiny winding street in Beverly Hills, around a few corners from the legendary Pickfair estate, where the Duquettes were married in the early 1950s.

Duquette bought the property shortly after the wedding. His friends, underestimating Duquette's powers of design, believed it to be an unbuildable lot. But before long a Xanadu-like vision had arisen from the canyon below. Topped with spires and domes, carvings from Bali and Thailand, and found objects, a cluster of pavilions mingled with the luxuriant foliage and the sinuous trunks of giant eucalypti.

At first the house was virtually one big drawing room, with French doors opening onto a terrace and the canyon. This lofty space became a project to be worked on over a number of years. The Duquettes painted the ceiling with a motif that rotates around a vast Duquette-designed chandelier, introducing the grandeur of a Venetian ballroom. The ornamented curtains are of cloth dipped in gesso and plaster and then painted with a floral motif. An eighteenth-century Italian painted screen from the Villa Malaparte near Venice is mounted across one wall, its breadth emphasized by a sofa that stretches nearly the width of the room.

The bedrooms were inspired by the Imperial Palace in Peking. Rich Chinese carvings, fabrics, and mirrored surfaces—all outlined by colored braids and trims (a favorite Duquette device)—create a layered and textured Oriental atmosphere.

Attracted as a child by the pageantry of Asia, Duquette has made many trips to India, Hong Kong, Thailand, and Bali, filling Dawnridge, his San Francisco home, and his Malibu ranch with souvenirs of his voyages. Duquette's raw materials come from a wide variety of sources—the navy sales at nearby Port Hueneme have been a big favorite. His effects are achieved by overlaying and juxtaposing diverse elements according to his own sense of shape and color. To the visitor, the results can be a dizzying experience. "I think what I want is never to have the eye stopped," says Duquette. "I don't want someone to be able to complete their view in one look."

ABOVE: The house overlooks a ravine filled with pagodas, fantasy pavilions, and junglelike foliage. OPPOSITE: Figures from Indochina and Thailand, set against Chinese paneling, frame a couch with a view of the garden beyond in a corner of the master bedroom. The painted box in the foreground is by Annie Kelly.

ABOVE: A corner of the drawing room. ABOVE RIGHT: The doors to the bedroom, with silver niello knobs. Thai stands flank the doorway, holding Burmese temples and tassles. OPPOSITE, CLOCKWISE FROM TOP: The drawing room is dominated by a Duquette-designed chandelier and painted panels from the Villa Malaparte near Venice. The pelmet is made of fabric soaked in plaster and then painted. In the small entry hall, Beegle Duquette has painted the inside of the door with a footman in 18th-century livery, ready to usher in guests. A corner of the drawing room.

A HOUSE IN BEL AIR

BY WILLIAM HAINES

IN 1957, BILLY HAINES AND HIS PARTNER, Ted Graber, redesigned a 1920s Spanish Colonial mansion built by architect Roland Coate. The Spanish Colonial exterior of the house did not correspond with Haines's high-fashion tastes. In Graber's words, "We came in and removed the 'mantilla,' giving the house a Classical look." The interiors were mostly left unchanged, except cosmetically, where the Haines touch was interspersed with furniture collected by the current owner.

A dramatic new loggia was created at the back of the U-shaped house and covered with a trellis, which projects a dappled light onto surfaces below. This provides linked views across the other ends of the U, from the living room on one side to the dining room on the other.

Behind the house, Haines added a full-length colonnade opening onto a large lawn extending to an axially aligned pool and pool house, interpreted, says Graber, "as a Classical pavilion with the spirit of a folly." This is furnished in the style of the period, around a fireplace set in a glazed wall.

Since 1957, the owner has lived here without feeling the need for anything more than an occasional sprucing-up by Graber—an indication of Haines's skill in planning and good design.

ABOVE: The front courtyard and house, with its redesigned 1957 neoclassical facade by Haines. OPPOSITE: The loggia, which overlooks the terrace and garden, receives a dappled light from an overhead trellis.

ABOVE: A corner of the living room is furnished with Haines-designed table and chairs. ABOVE RIGHT: This view is across the loggia from the living room. RIGHT: Haines designed a new colonnade and loggia for the rear of the house.

ABOVE: The fabric canopy on the pool pavilion is held aloft by spears. LEFT: Haines designed the chairs for the interior of the pavilion.

THE DUCOMMON HOUSE

BY TONY DUQUETTE

THE BEL AIR HOME OF Charles and Palmer Gross Ducommon was decorated by Tony Duquette in the 1960s. The front door opens onto an entry hall enlivened by a row of cupboard doors faced with antique Chinese panels, a pair of Venetian chairs, and a Duquette-designed chandelier. The living room is defined by another, much larger Duquette chandelier, this one created from abalone shells. Each of the lights was designed to illuminate an individual shell.

Palmer Ducommon loved color. In the living room Duquette took cues from the two paintings that hung there—a Braque and a Klee—and designed furniture in matching hues. The effect was vibrant: red curtains framed the yellow upholstery, which was accented with a sweep of red and green cushions. A Modigliani painting in the library provided inspiration for the vivid greens and oranges Duquette chose for that room.

Duquette designed everything in the dining room. Palmer Ducommon was fond of abstract sculpture, so Duquette created a gilded, organically shaped console table and mirror, flanked by sunburst light fixtures. The "Queen of Diamonds," a costumed figure in the dining room window, was a gift from Duquette, one of his series of maquettes for *The Jest of Cards*, a ballet produced at the time in San Francisco.

Over the years the Ducommons assembled a large collection of Duquette's jewelry designs and the maquettes he produced for various operas and ballets. Not surprisingly, Duquette considered them among his favorite and most supportive clients.

ABOVE: All the furniture in the dining room was designed by Duquette.
OPPOSITE: Duquette's organically shaped console table resembles abstract scuplture.

ABOVE: The vibrant colors of the living room were chosen to match the paintings: the Klee can be seen on the end wall. RIGHT: A Braque hangs over the fireplace, seen from the entry area. The Duquette-designed chandelier is made of mother-of-pearl. FAR RIGHT: In the case is a Duquette-designed costume maquette for the San Francisco Ballet production of "The Jest of Cards." OPPOSITE: A painting by Modigliani hangs over the fireplace in the sitting room.

SORTILEGIUM

BY TONY DUQUETTE

SORTILEGIUM (LATIN FOR "ENCHANTMENT") used to give passersby in the Malibu mountains the sudden and unexpected vision of having arrived in Darjeeling or Angkor. That was until the fire of November 1993 destroyed what Tony Duquette had steadily and compulsively built up since he bought the site as raw land in the 1950s. Among the few remains from the fire are a pair of magnificent eighteenth-century entrance gates from Spain. These are flanked by streetlights from Copenhagen—purchased during a visit to Karen Blixen.

Originally planned as a refuge from his busy career in Los Angeles, Sortilegium evolved into a work in itself, a cascade of pavilions, pagodas, and exotic landscaping that drifted down the sloping hillside to Serrano Canyon below. The driveway, dipping sharply and following the spine of the hill, was flanked by elaborate pedestals. These held pagoda-shaped porcelain electrical conductors found at a telephone company's surplus sale. Small pavilions and structures embellished with fantastic shapes, both man-made and natural, continued on both sides of the driveway. Octagonal trellises from the set of *Kismet,* whole eighteenth-century shopfronts from Dublin, masses of reindeer antlers shipped from the Hearst Castle at San Simeon (the Duquettes were houseguests the final weekend before it went public), sets from MGM Westerns, and bits and pieces from famous buildings in Hollywood—all were elements of Sortilegium's complex landscape.

The newest pavilion, the ballroom, stood at the end of the driveway. Duquette had finally found a use for huge windows and shutters rescued from a demolished *hôtel particulier* in Paris, which he had kept in storage for more than forty years, utilizing them as exterior walls to great effect. The building was destroyed before it could be used.

The main house was in the middle of this labyrinth, hidden by flowering vines. Quite small and surrounded with semi-enclosed verandas that were hung with plants and bird cages, it had views out across a broad valley to the mountains and the Pacific Ocean beyond. The house was filled with an extraordinary variety of furniture, objects, and plants. "I have used anything that captured the quality I was seeking," Duquette explains, "whether I found it in the streets, in an attic, in the desert, or by the sea. I don't like to reproduce what already exists. I'd rather take a shell, a rock, a tree branch, and a plastic grille, and use them to create an angel, a chandelier, or the front of a house."

ABOVE: The conservatory includes sections from several old San Francisco Victorian houses. OPPOSITE: A pair of horses guards the entry to a pavilion, overlooked by Boney Mountain.

ABOVE LEFT: One of Duquette's "Angel" figures, created for the Los Angeles Bicentennial. ABOVE: The antlers that decorate this pavilion came from San Simeon. LEFT: The pagodalike fixtures in the "Here Come The Clowns" garden came from an electrical supply house. OPPOSITE: The pathway leading to Frogmore, the building where the Duquettes lived, was guarded by a pair of Indian soldiers.

OPPOSITE: The walls and roof of the tea pavilion were decorated with a variety of appliqué techniques. ABOVE LEFT: The cottage-like sitting room at Frogmore exudes coziness, with comfortable daybed, ornate armoire, and piles of books and magazines. A doorway leads through to the dining room and kitchen. ABOVE: A colonnade—rescued from a mansion in L.A.'s now-demolished Bunker Hill district and decorated with colorful cushions, rugs, and a chandelier of antlers from the deer at San Simeon—runs the length of the Horned Toad pavilion. LEFT: Folk art is displayed under a ceiling lined with Greek rag rugs in Frogmore's festive dining room and kitchen.

RECENT MODERNISM

DURING THE EARLY 1970S THE ASSUMPTION that Modernism and Revivalism were set in eternal opposition was challenged by the arrival of post-Modernism, a reaction to the sterile environment produced by landscapes of bland, faceless Modernist buildings.

The post-Modernists pasted classical motifs lifted from the dusted-off pages of architectural history books onto the facades of their buildings to provide enrichment and meaning. They were careful to temper these applications with Modernist underpinnings to distinguish their "knowing allusions" from the literal historical evocations of the more prosaic Revivalists. A victim of its own popularity (the rash of cartoonlike facades spread over shopping centers across America eventually became as tiresome as the blank boxes they replaced), post-Modernism faded from grace in the late 1980s.

During the late 1970s and early 1980s, while most architects elsewhere in the country were embracing post-Modernism, an adventurous group of young Los Angeles architects—which included Frank Gehry, Eric Moss, Morphosis, and Fred Fisher—produced a series of radical houses that attracted worldwide attention. Influenced by the real-life look of urban Los Angeles (especially its alleys and construction sites), these houses introduced a new vocabulary of materials combined with collagelike elevational design, creating an aesthetic based on the way a building looked in the process of construction rather than its finished cosmeticized form.

Since the mid-1980s, these architects have followed diverse paths. Frank Gehry graduated to bigger and more international projects, using richer materials and continuing his exploration of sculptural and metaphorical forms. The Schnabel House in Brentwood explores his ongoing theme of fragmentation. Most of Gehry's peers seem conventional by comparison. Richard Meier's Ackerberg House in Malibu is classical and patrician, while Ricardo Legorreta's Greenberg House introduces colors and forms evolved from the traditional walls of Mexico, and Arthur Erickson's beach house pursues familiar versions of Modernism.

A group of younger architects continue the Los Angeles tradition of designing innovative houses appropriate to the region. These include Schweitzer/ BIM, Mark Mack, Frank Israel, Hank Koning and Julie Eizenberg, Craig Hodgetts, and Ming Fung. However, there is no longer the excitement of the 1970s and early 1980s, when the "Freestyle" architects created a new architectural vocabulary for residences during a period of conservatism elsewhere. Today most of L.A.'s archi-

The entrance gallery of the Goldberg/Bean house, 1992, by Franklin Israel.

tects are relatively subdued. In place of a locally generated "movement," there is an expression of a richer, less doctrinaire version of Modernism. Historical allusions are evident and are likely to emanate from twentieth-century sources—Art Deco and the fifties—as well as from the distinctive form making of Schindler, Barragán, and Gehry.

Less conservative is Brian Murphy, who stands alone with his conceptual approach to design. Raised locally, he spent much of his childhood on the beach. His father was a construction administrator, and Murphy grew up surrounded by the tools of the building trade, sketching on the back of blueprints.

His first design commission, for photographer Philip Dixon, was featured on the cover of *Progressive Architecture* magazine. This vaulted him from, as he put it, "an obscure but happy little builder guy" to a high-profile designer and architect. Since then Murphy has attracted a long list of clients from the Hollywood music and entertainment industries, as well as designing a series of houses for himself.

While most architects leave fixtures and fittings out of their design brief, Murphy happily goes the extra mile and fashions coffee tables, light fixtures, and fireplaces for each project, usually from recycled materials as varied as hula-skirt sconces (for a beach house with surfing and Hawaiian references) and a coffee table made of logs bound by a steel hawser. Collectively these designs have become a large and original body of work, almost a social commentary. Seen in their intended location, they do not seem arbitrary: there is always a strong sense of narrative and context. Indeed, Paul Goldberger has said that "the juxtaposition is a conscious elevation of everyday objects to high-design status, but it is done with a certain relaxed, easy air."

Meanwhile John Lautner, now in his eighties, is still reworking earlier projects and adding to his inventory of "timeless" architecture.

BEACH HOUSE

BY ARTHUR ERICKSON
INTERIORS BY BARBARA BARRY

DESIGNED AS A QUIET WEEKEND RETREAT for a busy Los Angeles couple, this serenely elegant house by architect Arthur Erickson stands out from its cottagey neighbors in a quiet beach community just outside the city. The house maximizes the experience of sitting on a dune a hundred feet from the water's edge. Full-depth glazed panels, which slide away, and a reflecting pool are all that separate the sand-colored stone flooring from the beach beyond. An outdoor shower set on a stainless-steel pole intercepts beachgoers on their way back into the house, and wet footprints evaporate instantly on the limestone floor.

A giant portico hovers over the terrace, which serves both as an entry zone for visitors and as a multipurpose living area, screened by etched glass from the beach. Upstairs, the secondary bedrooms, set back from the ocean, open onto the terrace, which draws the view back into these inner recesses.

The house is a classic Miesian structure, with references also to Pierre Chareau's Maison de Verre in Paris, with its elegant infill walls of glass block. The steelwork has been painted white, a metaphor for maritime structures. Indeed, the terrace creates something of the sensation of being on a cruise ship, and the whole house has the pristine quality that one associates with nautical design.

The kitchen and bathrooms were designed by Erickson's partner, Francisco Kripacz; the rest of the interiors are the work of interior designer Barbara Barry. Barry's approach was both refined and sensual. Respecting the crisp simplicity of the spaces, she introduced built-in fixtures wherever possible. The warmth of sycamore, used for the upstairs finishes, is a perfect complement to the cool glass, metal, and stone already in place. Simple modern classic furniture by Donghia, Vicente Wolfe, and Barry herself is upholstered, as befits a beach house, in white cotton.

ABOVE: The Erickson-designed dining table is flanked by potted citrus trees at the rear of the courtyard. OPPOSITE: Sheltered by a giant portico and with direct access to the beach, the courtyard serves as an outdoor family room.

LEFT: Seen from the beach at dusk, the house glows like a giant lantern. Sliding glass panels open the living room and bedroom above to ocean breezes. Opaque glazed doors lead into the courtyard. To the left of these is a stainless-steel shower pedestal. TOP: The living room looks out over a small reflecting pool to dunes and the ocean. Barbara Barry based her colors on the setting and the architecture. Sofas and chair backs are covered in white cotton. ABOVE: Erickson's partner, Francisco Kripacz, designed the stainless-steel kitchen.

LEFT: Barry used sycamore for the bed and dressers in the voluptuous master bedroom. The linens are by Peter Reed. TOP: In the same room, Barry also designed cabinets, desk, and desk chair. ABOVE: A guest bedroom has its own clever "borrowed" view of the ocean.

THE ACKERBERG HOUSE

BY RICHARD MEIER

MALIBU IS A STRAGGLING RESIDENTIAL COMMUNITY that extends for twenty-five miles along the coast to the northwest of Los Angeles. Squeezed between the Santa Monica Mountains and the Pacific Ocean, it is part suburban, part rustic. Its residents either live on the beach on narrow lots that resemble a continuous residential strip, or pursue a more rustic ranch style in the canyons beyond.

The area is famous for its beaches and its movie star residents; less so for its architecture. In fact, there are few places in the world where the real estate is so expensive and yet looks so cheap. Malibu's really good houses can be counted, if not on one hand, certainly on two. So the recent addition of the Ackerberg house by Richard Meier is all the more welcome, even if its crisp white panels, sophisticated geometry, and aura of class seem out of place with the rough redwood siding and fake brick of its neighbors.

Meier agreed to the Ackerberg commission, his first in California, shortly before winning the competition to build the new Getty Museum in Los Angeles. A recipient of the Pritzker Award (the architectural equivalent of the Nobel Prize), he had established his reputation with a series of museums and private houses, all pristinely white and recalling the early 1920s buildings of Le Corbusier.

Like most of Malibu's waterfront properties, the Ackerberg house is sandwiched between the beach and the busy coast highway behind. Unlike other nearby houses, however, it has room to breathe; the owners enjoy the luxury of a double-width lot. The house is separated from its glass-and-steel entry vestibule by an expanse of grass and presents a familiar Meieresque vocabulary: an undulating curved wall (which wraps around the living space) is played against right-angled planes of glass and ceramic tile. Walls and floor plans conform to a grid module. As always with Meier, the building's color is strictly white.

The living area is built around a cube-shaped central volume, delineated by columns and extending to the roof, where a continuous clerestory floods the room with light. The exterior walls (curved to the rear and fully glazed to the side and oceanfront) are aligned beyond the columns as a nonstructural membrane. Granite paving, used inside and out, also lines the swimming pool. An exterior *brise-soleil* protects the interior from the sun while allowing light and shadows to play across the exterior, adding a sense of layering to the beach elevation.

ABOVE: The master bedroom is a tranquil essay in Modernism. OPPOSITE: The rear of the living room, seen from the entry courtyard. The house is entered through a colonnade to the right.

ABOVE: To the side of the house is "Fountain Figure," a sculpture by Robert Graham. BELOW: The living room is double-height. Column supports are set in from each corner and the roof is pushed up to admit light through a wraparound clerestory. Furnishings are by interior designer Tim Morrison. RIGHT: The front elevation overlooks a granite-paved pool and a view of the beach.

THE BEYER BEACH HOUSE

BY JOHN LAUTNER

NESTLED INTO LECHUSA POINT, a rocky headland northwest of Malibu, this Lautner project was designed as a beach house for Lynn and Stanley Beyer, but it became their permanent home. Built on a triple lot, the house enjoys one of the best oceanfront sites between Santa Barbara and Laguna.

The two-story free-form house is covered by a swooping roof of concrete. A spectacular living room, with a curved mezzanine hovering over the rear of the space, overlooks rocks, seagulls, and crashing surf. The roof dips protectively toward the water, focusing views downward to the ocean's expanse and protecting the interior from the late afternoon sun. Exterior terraces are sheltered from breezes and rough seas by plate-glass screens. Around the corner, set into a sheltered terrace and nestling under a curved protective concrete canopy, is a swimming pool. The canopy, its owner says, "makes you feel as though you're swimming inside a wave."

The organic theme is continued inside: giant boulders were incorporated into the design of the living room and in places function as furniture. Lautner collaborated with interior designer Michael Taylor to create living areas that reflect Taylor's love of natural elements and overscale forms.

The organic form of the house, and Lautner's sensitively bold design, invite a level of participation in an extraordinary environment which a more conventional plan based on rectangles and picture-window openings could never achieve.

ABOVE: The Beyer house is nestled into Lechusa Point, north of Malibu. Note the downward swoop of the roof. OPPOSITE: The living room almost seems to hover over the surf. The downward curve of the roof directs the eye to the drama outside. Furnishings, arranged around giant rocks brought in from central California, are by Michael Taylor.

JOSHUA TREE

BY SCHWEITZER/BIM

THIS WEEKEND RETREAT WAS DESIGNED by architect Josh Schweitzer for himself and four friends. It sits on ten acres of rocky landscape in the high desert between the town of Joshua Tree and the nearby Joshua Tree National Monument.

The region, devoid of style statements or of anything resembling architecture, is a perfect antidote to everyday life in Hollywood. The indigenous environment consists of drab, bunkerlike buildings aspiring to nothing more than survival against a harsh climate. Cacti, abandoned vehicles, TV satellite dishes, and the spiky, primeval Joshua trees—all are dwarfed by the immensity of the terrain. There is a suggestion of the postapocalyptic novels of J. G. Ballard, and of Mad Max movies.

Because of its bright colors, the house is visible from afar, but it offers very little sense of scale, especially as many of the surrounding rocks are the same size as the house. This has a miniaturizing effect. At the same time, its dominance in the landscape, due to its strong forms and colors, gives the house a sense of being a monument.

The complex is designed in simple, cubist shapes. The interiors have been kept simple as befits a wilderness retreat, though more built-in furniture is planned. Openings cut into the exterior forms give the effect from within of being, as Schweitzer says, "inside a cave in the rocks. The windows and doors are the crevices that frame the view."

TOP: The complex, with a Joshua tree in the foreground, is designed in simple cubist shapes and skewed angles; a living pavilion in olive green is attached to a royal blue bedroom wing; the orange-red structure is the gazebo. ABOVE: Light pours into the simple interior from a variety of irregularly shaped windows and door openings. OPPOSITE: The house and its surroundings.

GREENBERG HOUSE

BY RICARDO LEGORRETA

RICARDO LEGORRETA, IN A RECENT MONOGRAPH on his work published by the University of Texas, wrote: "Usually I dream of color, walls, mystery, intimacy, and other qualities that matter to me as a person, and as a Mexican." The entry courtyard of his new Greenberg residence, one of the most dramatic spaces in Los Angeles, is a place where his dreams have become a reality. Designed for Audrey and Arthur Greenberg on a quiet street, it exhibits a patrician presence.

Walls are the predominant element in the architecture of Mexico; here they are massive, inscrutable, seductively colored, and perforated by discreet openings that suggest rather than reveal activities within. A group of eighty-foot palm trees rising from a gravel base adds drama to the entry courtyard.

The interior, floored with limestone, is quiet, serene, and comfortably furnished. Drama is added by a reflecting pool that separates the entry passage from the breakfast room and by a hot-pink skylight that hovers over the stairs. Large windows and French doors frame a landscaped back garden; its jacarandas, yuccas, and coral trees were transplanted from the Greenbergs' previous garden.

TOP: The stairwell and a skylight with hot-pink louvers. ABOVE: The entry courtyard is one of the most dramatic outdoor spaces in the city. OPPOSITE: A lavender-painted interior courtyard with a fountain—behind the glass wall to the right—separates the entry passage from the breakfast room and fills it with color and the sound of splashing water.

THE HOPPER STUDIO

BY BRIAN MURPHY

DENNIS HOPPER'S RESIDENTIAL STUDIO is in a part of Venice noted more for its gang activity than for its proximity to the beach. Designing the studio in 1988, with security high on his priority list, Murphy created a fortified enclave elegantly sheathed in corrugated metal. A picket fence left by the previous owners was reinstated in front as a visual tie-in with the studio's raffish surroundings.

Despite its lack of windows the interior is light and airy, thanks to a series of skylights set into a vast wave-shaped roof. It is also luxurious. The first floor was designed as a work and storage area, with a theater/rehearsal studio, gallery space for Hopper's extensive art collection, and a garage at the back. Stairs lead up to a lofty living area, over which the roof describes an enveloping curve, adding texture with its exposed wood frame. Several Murphy touches enliven the space: a fireplace with a trough of smashed auto glass, coffee tables made of upended eucalyptus logs, and a suspended glass-disc chandelier, its light sources buried beneath more auto glass. Antique furniture from the Mabel Dodge Luhan estate in Taos, where Hopper lived in the seventies, and paintings from the Hopper collection, flesh out the space.

TOP: Seen from the rear alley, the roof of the Hopper studio undulates like a wave. ABOVE: The loft-like upper living space is lit by skylights. Table and chairs to the right are from the Mable Dodge Luhan estate in Taos. OPPOSITE: The inscrutable front facade. Murphy retained the property's existing white picket fence.

ABOVE: Inset against a window of sandwiched layers of glass—the middle layer fractured with a hammer—is the fireplace, which sits in a trough that echoes the shape of the window and is filled with shattered auto glass. To the left of the fireplace is a Duchamp ready-made. The coffee table is made of logs on casters, fitted with glass covers. RIGHT: Beyond this corner of the master bedroom is the bathroom. OPPOSITE: The all-glass bathtub was fabricated by Murphy's frequent collaborator, Simon Maltby.

SUMMERS RESIDENCE

BY MARK MACK

THE ANDY AND KATE SUMMERS HOME in Santa Monica was designed by architect Mark Mack, a recent transplant to L.A. from San Francisco. As with his earlier Bay Area houses, Mack has combined simple forms with a distinctive graphic approach and use of color. Since he arrived from Vienna in 1973, this Austrian-born architect has developed a distinctive version of Modernism, one that owes more to a personal interpretation of primitive building than to central Modernist themes.

The plan of the Summers house was partially inspired by the work of Austrian pioneer Modernist Adolph Loos, reflecting the latter's interest in primitive multistoried Moroccan dwellings—flat-roofed structures with exterior steps leading to roof terraces.

Reversing the familiar suburban configuration seen on the rest of the street, Mack placed the house at the back of the lot, with a studio for Andy Summers at the front of the site. This creates a private courtyard garden, overlooked by the house and its attached terrace.

An entry loggia next to the studio frames a first view of the house at the end of an attractively paved and landscaped path (by landscape designer Nancy Goslee Power). An outdoor living area, raised above the lawn, forms a natural extension of the family room and kitchen, whose glazed doors fold away completely. This outdoor living space is provided with a fireplace and grill for outdoor dining. A flight of stairs ascends, Moroccan-style, to a separate, upstairs patio, which

is connected by more foldaway doors to a family room with bedrooms beyond.

Andy Summers is a musician (he was a member of the rock group The Police), and an artist, while Kate is a psychiatrist, and they have three children. The house accommodates a variety of activities requiring varying degrees of privacy. Mack provided rooms of varying shapes and heights which, with linking stairs and steps, result in a rich and complex environment.

ABOVE: An entry loggia, next to the studio, frames a first view of the house, which is glimpsed at the end of an atractive path and garden (by landscape designer Nancy Goslee Power). OPPOSITE: An outdoor living area, raised a few steps above the lawn, forms a natural extension of the family room and kitchen (through fold-away glazed doors to the left), and is provided with a fireplace and grill for outdoor dining. Steps ascend, Moroccan-style, to a separate, upstairs patio with access to the upstairs family rooms.

ABOVE AND RIGHT: Mack used color-stained concrete for the floor in the bathroom and elsewhere, a local tradition dating back to Irving Gill. Its deep, lustrous, waxed finish complements the stained ash woodwork and primary-colored ceramic tiles, and creates an impression that the house has evolved over time.

LEFT: Olive-green woodwork delineates the staircase, seen from the upstairs family room. BELOW: An informal dining area with a Mack-designed banquette is adjacent to the kitchen.

SCHNABEL HOUSE

BY FRANK GEHRY

MARINA AND ROCKWELL SCHNABEL'S new Brentwood home is a residential version of Frank Gehry's continued experiments with architectural fragmentation, seen to good effect in his villagelike campus for Loyola Law School near downtown Los Angeles. As with several earlier residences, the house is not a single building in which all activities are sheltered under one encompassing roof. Instead, it has become a sculptural composition of individual elements, each treated in a distinctive way, or, as Gehry himself comment, "objects placed in the landscape like a Morandi still life." Entered through a copper-sheathed gate, the Schnabel residence is revealed as a group of discrete buildings in a landscaped environment, each one shaped and clad differently from the next.

The separate parts of the house have been pushed out to the edges of the site to create a "village." Individual structures are connected by informally shaped patios and courtyards, all making the property seem much larger than it is. Gehry also encouraged the owners to personalize individual buildings. "This allows the clients more involvement," says Gehry, "because you can say, 'Well, I've got ten images now that are going to compose your house; these images can relate to all kinds of symbolic things, ideas you have liked, bits and pieces of your life you would like to recall.'"

A path of California sandstone leads toward a centrally placed living pavilion, through landscaping designed by Nancy Goslee Power. On the left is a stand of arid-zone flowers set against the side wall of the garage. On the right is an olive grove, beyond which, heralded by copper-clad columns, is Rockwell Schnabel's study. This is topped by a copper-sheathed dome, a reference to Marina Schnabel's visits to the Griffith Observatory as a child. The olive trees represent the city's first olives, planted below the observatory at the turn of the century near Olive Hill (site of Wright's Hollyhock House). The office interior is a square volume with a copper-sheathed fireplace. The interior of the dome high overhead is finished in smooth plaster.

The cruciform living pavilion is placed centrally and anchors the whole composition. Its interior is furnished with couches designed by Marina Schnabel, who trained as an architect and worked for a time in the Gehry office. Above this is a central campanilelike tower, which draws light into the space below and successfully convects heat out through its high-level vents. To one side of the space is the dining area, and to the other is a more intimate sunken area set around a copper-clad fireplace.

The kitchen and family rooms are placed together in a plain box-like structure, which acts as a foil for the dramatic architecture around it. Then, set at the back of the property below a massive retaining wall, the master bedroom sits like a boat moored on a lake, evoking Finnish landscapes (Rockwell Schnabel was ambassador to Finland). The bedroom structure is surmounted by a sculptural skylight, its supports suggesting tree trunks (another memory of Finland). The large pylons emerging from the water provide shade from the direct early-morning sun. The refusal to make the lake "picturesque" by adding rocks, water plants, and fish emphasizes the rigorously conceptual nature of Gehry's architecture.

The copper-clad colonnade links the garage with the kitchen.

ABOVE: Inside the front courtyard, the village-like arrangement is anchored by the central living pavilion, clad in lead-coated copper. To the left is the white-stuccoed kitchen/family room wing, and to the right is the copper-domed office pavilion. The landscaping, with a lush border on the left and an olive grove on the right, is by Nancy Goslee Power. RIGHT: To the right of the tiled lap pool is the living pavilion.

LEFT: The master bedroom pavilion, resembling a barge, sits in a lake surrounded by protective copper pylons. The rest of the house, with a studio pavilion to the left, is on the upper level. Facing the water below is a passage that links the master bedroom with bathrooms and a gym. BELOW LEFT: The office pavilion, its dome evoking memories of the Griffith Park Observatory. BELOW: The living pavilion, with its campanile-like tower, is a focal point for the whole complex.

LEFT: Interior of the cruciform living pavilion, topped by a central tower with skylights and windows that frame a solitary palm. The view is from the dining space looking toward a central seating area, with a more intimate grouping around the copper-clad fireplace beyond. The lap pool can be glimpsed through the end windows. Furnishings by Marina Schnabel and natural finishes in wood and copper add warmth to the space.
ABOVE: A copper-clad coat closet, which opens from the back, stands to the right of the glazed entry door.

CONTEMPORARY DECORATING

AT JARRETT HEDBORG'S INITIAL MEETING with his first major client, Jack Nicholson crumpled an old fedora in his hand and lobbed it into a chair, exclaiming, "I want my house to look like that, Jarrett." With these words, Hedborg was initiated into the often unpredictable world of Los Angeles decorating.

Decorators such as Waldo Fernandez, Barbara Barry, Tom Callaway, Linda Marder, and Brian Murphy work hard at interpreting the private dreams of an eclectic group of movie stars, directors, producers, and studio bosses. As Brad Gooch wrote, "Decorators to the stars turn the stuff of such dreams—often expressed in a client's chance phrase or a photo ripped from a magazine [or a crumpled

fedora]—into just the right celadon screening room, or long red swimming pool, or hillside of cactus and pepper trees."

The Hollywood glamour of the 1930s, '40s, and '50s is gone. The tuxedoed Gary Coopers have been replaced by stars of a more casual breed, sporting T-shirts and Armani jackets. The stars today no longer get dressed up and ride around in convertibles acknowledging their fans with a gracious wave, or wear evening dress to every dinner party, as they did in the 1950s. Nonetheless, they aspire to a home style as chic as the cars they drive and the clothes they wear.

While decorating for the entertainment industry is perhaps the most conspicuous story here, it is not the only one. Many of the houses in this chapter, for instance, are those of the decorators themselves, full of personal idiosyncrasies and serving as laboratories for the owners' developing ideas. "California's only real tradition is change," said decorator Stephen Shubell, and this applies to the interior styles of L.A.'s uniquely eclectic houses and apartments.

San Franciscan Michael Taylor was one of the most successful California decorators. He worked in a variety of styles, and his later work was an influence on such younger southern California designers as Kalef Alaton and Waldo Fernandez. Inspired by Japanese landscape design and a sense of nature, Taylor used overscale natural elements—rocks, wood, and wicker—set against white plastered walls.

The revival of historical styles is still a popular theme in Los Angeles, and a group of younger designers and decorators have emerged who employ a Mediterranean influence as inspiration for their work. This is a thread that has run through Los Angeles design since the Spanish first re-created their monasteries and churches in the New World of California.

Recycled influences from Latin America also return to give added richness to contemporary interiors. Waldo Fernandez, who inherited the oversize, white-on-white look Michael Taylor made famous, later discarded this for a more personal Latin approach, which reflected his Cuban heritage. His work can be dramatic, and he has been called the master of the big effect.

Artists have always been tempted to develop their own surroundings. Influenced by frequent trips to Mexico, Annie Kelly renovated her own Hollywood hills Spanish Revival house in the mid-1980s, using friezes and vivid color to give the house character. Jarrett Hedborg has a very Californian sense of light and color, and he too frequently introduces friezes and hand-painted designs, resulting from collaborations with decorative painter Nancy Kintisch. Hedborg

TOP: An elegant console made from a found Coca-Cola chest topped by a composition-stone slab anchors a wall in landscape designer Jay Griffith's dining room.
ABOVE: A couch by designer Larry Totah is used in the living room of his own house.

enjoys designing in a variety of styles, not least the romantic evocation of Hawaii, which runs through his own house with bright flashes of blues and yellows.

Hutton Wilkinson, who worked for Tony Duquette for many years, has inherited the mantle of the Hollywood decorators of the past. His own house, which is furnished with period and antique European furniture, displays the same vivid sense of color, style, and creativity the early Hollywood set decorators employed when they created the fabulous backdrops for such movies as *Marie Antoinette.*

Rose Tarlow, antiquarian, furniture designer, and occasional interior designer—"but only to her friends"—has an almost legendary reputation. She operates from her Melrose House store in West Hollywood and is traditional in her approach, but her work is personal and difficult to categorize. Her own home, a study in creams and browns, is a refined version of a classic California rancho.

While not a decorator himself, antiquarian Gep Durenberger has influenced many L.A. designers directly and indirectly—through his Decorative Arts Study Center in San Juan Capistrano,

TOP: This informal dining table is in the home of Rachel Ashwell, who runs the Shabby Chic store in Santa Monica. ABOVE: The master bedroom of a house Roy McMakin decorated in Brentwood for Peter and Barbara Benedekuses features McMakin-designed furniture. OPPOSITE: Architect/designer Brian Murphy's own living room in Santa Monica shows his versatility with recycled elements; in this case, a coffee table fashioned of bound logs and a cluster of crimson-sprayed chandeliers.

and by inviting decorators to visit and study his own 1920s cottage. Its eighteenth-century ambience was enhanced by the addition of period doors and windows shipped over from Europe.

The theme of Modernism still runs through decorating today. Barbara Barry's work epitomizes a contemporary, quietly elegant sense of luxury, based on simplicity and quality materials and comfort. Her own house, with its dark wood, cream silk, and Moderne architecture, has the feel of a Cedric Gibbons movie set.

Linda Marder is the true professional, working in a variety of styles. She moves easily from a country cottage for actress Teri Garr to serious Modernism for producer Ron Meyer to 1920s Frank Lloyd Wright for producer Joel Silver.

L.A.'s decorators and designers work in a broad spectrum of styles from traditional to radical, making it as difficult as ever to categorize this most culturally diversified of cities. One of the best things about living in Los Angeles is the ability to reinvent yourself, to appropriate a background from the plethora of possibilities available in this great marketplace of styles.

ROSE TARLOW'S OWN HOUSE

ROSE TARLOW HAS RUN THE MELROSE HOUSE SHOP in West Hollywood for nearly twenty years, selling a range of her own furniture in a variety of antique and modern styles. Her first love is chair design, and she is obsessive about proportion: "Many antiques are poorly proportioned and aesthetically unimportant." Her furniture reinterprets classic Chippendale, Regency, and other styles, reshaping the originals until they meet her vision of good design. Her favorite chairs can be from all periods, grand or humble in origin. Simple vernacular designs are high on the list.

Many of her best chairs find their way into Tarlow's idiosyncratic residence in Bel Air, where they take their place among cream-colored upholstered furniture, ancient objects of wood and iron, and twentieth-century drawings. Her lofty living room is lined with vellum-bound books and green vines that cascade romantically down the walls.

The house is architecturally quite simple, like an early California rancho, and is intended to provide a neutral background for Tarlow's collections.

ABOVE: The garden of Rose Tarlow's wisteria and Virginia creeper–decked house in Beverly Hills. Comfortably upholstered furniture from Melrose House provides a setting for tea. OPPOSITE: An outdoor dining area in Tarlow's garden with an 18th-century French stone table, partially encircled by a crescent-shaped stone seat with cushions.

OPPOSITE: In the guest bedroom, an 18th-century French bed folds up to form a settee. TOP: In the same room, a desk faces a view of the garden. ABOVE: Tarlow describes her rooms as "backgrounds for objects I adore." To the left of the stone fireplace is a pair of 17th-century English library chairs.

WALDO FERNANDEZ'S OWN HOUSE

THE COMPACT HOUSE OF DECORATOR WALDO FERNANDEZ sits enigmatically behind aged terra-cotta walls on Sunset Boulevard as it winds through Beverly Hills.

Approached through an entry courtyard paved with Mexican tile and landscaped with stone and terra-cotta planters, the house, which has the scale of a classic French pavilion, gives the impression of understated luxury and comfort. Mexican tile is used outdoors and in, where a high passageway extends the length of the house, ending in a small sitting area and fireplace. The passage is lit by a series of French doors opening onto a patio, which is defined by an elegantly simple swimmimg pool edged by square planters filled with lavender.

Inside, the walls are a creamy off-white that blends well with the beige linens and sisal rugs. Occasionally Fernandez interjects a note of pattern: a fragment of gold Fortuny cotton damask or a muted stripe.

The entry courtyard of the Fernandez house, with a view along the hallway.

OPPOSITE, CLOCKWISE FROM TOP LEFT: An overscale lantern hangs in a corner of the rear courtyard. In a small sitting room at the end of the main passage, Fernandez-designed cotton-upholstered chairs face a neoclassical German 18th-century desk and English Regency chair. The dining table is covered with 19th-century fabric and surrounded by French Directoire chairs; the chandelier is 17th-century Portuguese. Early Philippine jars and large fossils are grouped on the mantel. The living room is beyond. Light floods into the hallway from the rear courtyard. The two small chairs facing each other at the end are French Louis XVI from Versailles and are signed by Jacob. The floor is Mexican tile. ABOVE: The master bedroom is crisp and elegant, with elements perfectly scaled for the room. On the left is an 18th-century Chinese lacquered cabinet. The bed canopy, the upholstery of the Fernandez-designed chairs, and the draperies are all of cream-colored cotton.

BARBARA BARRY'S OWN HOUSE

INTERIOR DESIGNER BARBARA BARRY LIVES in a moderately sized and finely detailed 1930s Moderne-style duplex in the Fairfax district. The well-tailored house suits Barry's reflective and well-thought-out home life. The stuccoed walls and Moderne detailing of the interior evoke glamorous 1930s movies, conjuring images of cream silk charmeuse dresses and long black cigarette holders tipped with silver.

Barry reminds us that when it comes to the art of living well, real luxury exists only on an intimate scale, encompassed by what you can touch. "I'm not wealthy, but I treat myself the way a good hotel treats me," she stated in a recent interview. "I've got the best sheets, the best shower head, and a silver tray. When I come home, I'll make tea, put it on the tray, and go sit in the bathtub and read."

Barry's chief inspiration has been from the influential French decorator of the 1930s Jean-Michel Frank, who also believed in the luxury of simple forms and good materials.

RIGHT: A composition of forms—crisp cotton thrown over an ottoman, a slender mirror, a mannequin, and an antique armoire—create a scenario of their own in Barry's bedroom. OPPOSITE: One of Barry's signature star lamps—this one from London—forms a counterpoint to a serene bedside in carefully muted colors. Morning sunlight filters across the celadon wallpaper, mirrored table, and voluptuous bed-linens.

ABOVE: The sitting room doubles as a library. Barry designed her desk, which she describes as "Elsie de Wolfe meets Jean-Michel Frank," with large-scale fluting to echo the box-pleating on the chairs (another Barry signature). ABOVE RIGHT: An arch, evocative of 1930s glamour, frames a small table in the passage. The door opens into a studio. RIGHT: A paper lantern floats over the round dining table, surrounded by Barry's 1930s-inspired pleated, slip-covered chairs. Glazed doors with white linen curtains open onto a small terrace. OPPOSITE: A Sally Gall photograph, a silver dish, and a chromed lamp create a 1930s grouping on a Deco rosewood table in the sitting room.

WALKER/SHEFFIELD HOUSE

BY BRIAN MURPHY

POET CYNTHIA WALKER AND COMEDY SCREENWRITER David Sheffield were already Murphy fans when they hired him to renovate their Hollywood Lake cottage (once owned by singer Ruth Etting). "I saw Brian Murphy as a designer with a wonderful comic sense," says Sheffield. "Not everybody can create a dining room chandelier of police flashlights and broken windshield glass."

Murphy opened up the entry hall, the staircase to the lower floor, and the living room to create a large open space punctuated by the newly exposed brick structure of the chimney, which rises next to the stairs. Lighting and a sense of brightness was a focus of the remodeling. New windows and skylights were installed, together with a wood floor lacquered silver. The room was furnished with a Dakota Jackson club chair upholstered in silver leather, and silver-painted tables make the open-plan living area gleam and shine. Visitors are greeted by a constellation of eighteen white powder-coated chandeliers grouped around the chimney and over the stairs. At night the multitude of candles perched on every available surface lights up the house. In the bathroom Murphy again plays with light, contrasting dainty crystal chandeliers with a pair of rearview truck mirrors, placed over the basin. For the dining room he created a chandelier with a sheet of plate glass supporting votive candles, suspended over a delicate dining room table by a set of black pipe clamps.

ABOVE: In the dining room Murphy created a chandelier from a sheet of plate glass and an array of votive candles, suspended over the dining table by a set of black pipe clamps. OPPOSITE: The marquee-like entry lobby, covered with a canvas awning and with canvas curtains on each side, gives a note of mock formality to a quiet street in the Hollywood hills.

ABOVE LEFT: The living room floor was painted silver and then covered with a clear lacquer. The occasional tables are also painted silver. ABOVE: For the powder room Murphy combined a basin fitted on—instead of into—a marble countertop, mirrors from a truck-parts catalog, and crystal chandeliers. LEFT: Existing living room walls were removed, transforming the living room, stairwell, and entry hall into a single volume. The chimney now stands, surrounded by a mesmerising array of white powder-coated chandeliers, as a sculptural object in the space. OPPOSITE: In the master bedroom, a 19th-century French bed is transformed into a four-poster with steel columns and curtains with a metallic sheen.

OYLER HOUSE

BY BRIAN MURPHY

BRIAN MURPHY WAS INVITED BY Michelle and Connolly Oyler to "rescue" the somewhat unprepossessing mansion they had just bought in Pacific Palisades. As Murphy recalls, "I was confronted with a big old house, in a sort of antebellum-Delta-typico style, sitting on a hill. There was no way to hide it, so I decided to remove the hedge that screened it from the street and open it up." Murphy graded the front yard to give a rolling lawn effect and put in a picket fence and a formal front entry framed by cast-iron jockeys, transforming it into a pristine southern mansion.

The house itself is full of Murphy-designed incidents, beginning with the scarlet-laquered entry hall. The formal moment of entry—with the initial greetings, the coats being taken by the hosts, and the ushering through to the rest of the house—is made into a memorable one.

RIGHT: The Oylers' scarlet-laquered entry hall and staircase prepare visitors for the unexpected. OPPOSITE: Despite its starchy antebellum facade, jockeys, white picket fence, and green lawns, the Oyler house is not as conservative as it seems. The '57 Chevy convertible parked in the driveway once belonged to Steve McQueen.

OPPOSITE: Scarlet footprints along a linoleum-clad passage follow the dogs' route to and from the backyard door. ABOVE: A jelly-mold chandelier designed by Heidi Wianeki hangs over the breakfast table. ABOVE RIGHT: The living room is reflected in a mirror over the mantel. RIGHT: Living-room track lighting from low-voltage lamps is carried on mobile bogeys from a Lionel train set. The track, which channels the electricity, is suspended from the ceiling.

TOM BEETON'S OWN HOUSE

DECORATOR TOM BEETON APPRENTICED with Gep Duren-berger, the noted San Juan Capistrano antiquarian, then opened his own antiques store on La Cienega in West Hollywood. Three years later he became design director at Ralph Lauren. This gave him a broad stylistic range. Now working on his own, Beeton has a wide variety of clients.

In his own apartment, in a 1936 Streamline Moderne building in Hancock Park, Beeton experiments with various design ideas. Subtle wall finishes provide a variety of atmospheric backgrounds for an eclectic but carefully matched assortment of furniture spanning three centuries.

An entry door with a small porthole window opens directly into the living room, where 1920s French club chairs mingle with Robsjohn Gibbings chairs from the 1950s, a Louis Philippe–style sofa (thought to be a movie prop), and a plaster-swagged table designed by Beeton, overlooked by an eighteenth-century mirror. The glazed walls by Elloree Findley are finished with an undulating striation that matches the Moderne curves of the walls. An inexpensive silver gilt, glazed for a rich effect, was used for the mantelpiece.

Evident everywhere is a rich variety of texture and surface: rattan, old leather, lacquer, gilt, Fortuny cotton, white piqué, animal-print velvet, and hand-beaded pillows. Beeton calls it his "Chanel principle," a penchant for mixing costly and cheap. His design is a good example of the contemporary European influence in L.A., the return to traditional interiors with a twist.

ABOVE: In a corner of the bedroom: a painting of Beeton's previous studio by Julian Latrobe is propped on a 19th-century French Gothic chair—with fringe added by Beeton. Beside the bed, and piled with books and mementos, is an English William IV what-not. OPPOSITE: A Hispano-Mooresque dado painted by Dana Westring in an aged pomegranate color gives the bedroom a romantic fin-de-siècle aura. A William IV giltwood armchair, slip-covered love seat, and mirror from a 1930s movie palace provide a lively mix of furnishings.

LEFT: Subtle wall finishes in the living room provide atmospheric backgrounds for an eclectic but carefully matched assortment of furniture spanning three centuries. The glazed walls, painted by Elloree Findley, are finished with an undulating striation that matches their Moderne curves. An inexpensive silver gilt, also glazed for a rich effect, was used for the mantelpiece. Two 1920s French club chairs mingle with a Louis Philippe-style sofa (thought to have been a movie prop), and a Robsjohn Gibbings chair from the 1950s stands in front of a plaster swagged table designed by Beeton. The mirror is an 18th-century piece. ABOVE: Artist Dana Westring's Italian urns line the dining room walls, which were painted gray and stenciled with dots and ribbons. Dining chairs were upholstered by Beeton with antique crystal tassels.

JARRETT HEDBORG'S OWN HOUSE

JARRETT HEDBORG'S TRAINING AS AN ARTIST has led to a more painterly and deliberately idiosyncratic approach than those of most design-trained decorators. His diverse client list includes, in addition to Nicholson, Bette Midler and her husband, director Martin von Haselberg, Jeff Bridges, Anjelica Huston, Joni Mitchell, Quincy Jones, and Michelle Phillips.

For his own house Hedborg was able to indulge in his personal romance with the islands of Hawaii. Bold patterns form a background for his collection of nineteenth-century engravings of fish and birds, Japanese prints, and a spectacular swordfish in midleap over the fireplace. Hawaiian music wafts gently through the rooms, as if carried in by friendly trade winds.

ABOVE: A pineapple lamp, a 19th-century bird print, and an assortment of color-related objects are arranged on a desk in the living room. OPPOSITE: The South Seas theme continues in the sitting room. The handwoven Lahala mat is from Fiji; the coffee table with woven raffia finish is from the Philippines. The pillows are made of pareu fabric. The paintings are by Harry Carmen. OVERLEAF LEFT: The wall next to the indigo-and-white tiled fireplace was stenciled with Hawaiian plant patterns by artist Nancy Kintisch. OVERLEAF RIGHT, CLOCKWISE FROM TOP LEFT: Kintisch painted the alcove; the chrome lithographs and Polynesian-fantasy painting are from the 19th century. In the bedroom, a Hedborg-designed chair in blue and white ticking sits in front of Hawaiian-print curtains; the pillow is covered with linen from Hedborg's Swedish great-grandparents' wedding. The chair in this Kintisch-painted entry near the kitchen is covered in Fortuny fabric. In the dining room a gilded chair is covered with Tahitian pareu and a Hawaiian plaid; 18th-century Japanese wood-block prints contrast with the boldly painted wall pattern by Kintisch.

THE BETTE MIDLER HOUSE

BY JARRETT HEDBORG

JARRETT HEDBORG'S TRANSFORMATION of a 1920s Mediterranean villa in Bel Air is one of his more colorful projects. The house of actress and singer Bette Midler, her husband, director Martin von Haselberg, and their daughter, Sophie, it resembles a stroll through the pages of a sophisticated children's book, with a bright blend of colorful elements and delicately painted surfaces. Artist Nancy Kintisch painted and stenciled most wall surfaces in the house, some of the floors as well, and a frieze that wraps around the exterior, a project that took many months. A variety of patterns and motifs was applied, including a diaphanous trompe l'oeil curtain pulled back from a (real) window, painted so faintly that the effect is almost subliminal. Walls that at first sight seem blank reveal their secrets upon closer inspection.

The living room is extensive, broken up with chair groupings for intimate conversation and layered with bright patterns, books, and flowers. Colors get stronger in the main bedroom, a rustic Middle-European fantasy with a brightly painted folk-art fireplace and a Macintosh-inspired bed. Von Haselberg's own room sets a different mood; with a collection of artifacts and light fixtures by artist friends, it is more masculine and conceptual.

This house was inspired by two houses that Midler had always liked: the extensively painted and influential home of the Swedish artist Carl Larsson and the exuberantly hand-painted Charleston, the English country home of Bloomsbury artists Vanessa Bell and Duncan Grant.

TOP: Artist Nancy Kintisch painted the chairs against the end wall and the almost subliminal wall and ceiling decorations in the living room. ABOVE: The sitting room is enlivened by floral prints; the wall decorations are by Kintisch. OPPOSITE: Colors are stronger in the master bedroom, a rustic Middle-European fantasy with a brightly painted folk-art fireplace.

TWO INTERIORS

BY ANNIE KELLY

ANNIE KELLY HAS BEEN INFLUENCED by sources as diverse as early California missions and Mexican interiors. She uses walls of strong color and furniture of her own design to give an individual look to her work. Like Jarrett Hedborg, Kelly trained in art rather than design.

Annie Kelly, together with the author, moved into a 1920s Southwestern-style house in the Hollywood hills at the beginning of the 1980s. Inspired by visits to Mexico—in particular, to Frida Kahlo's house in Coyoacan—she designed interiors with a Mexican theme for the house. Widely published, these designs helped pioneer a Mexican trend in decorating, which developed during the decade. In the same period, Kelly also decorated a sitting room in her nearby studio, using painted surfaces to give personality to a tiny space.

ABOVE RIGHT: Kelly decorated the small entry/sitting room of her studio with motifs inspired by Picasso on cupboard doors and echoed on a 1940s glass-topped table. The chairs are from Mexico. RIGHT: Kelly painted the wall to give it an aged look and added a pencil-thin dado. The table was partially stripped and left unpainted to give it a patina of age. The glass jug and retablo are from Mexico. OPPOSITE: In the Hollywood hills house, curtains form a division between the dining and sitting rooms, which are otherwise unified by a painted dado. The dining table, with 1950s Oriental pottery from Vallauris, was designed and made by Kelly. The Barbarian chair is by Garouste and Bonetti.

TWO PROJECTS

BY TOM CALLAWAY

TOM CALLAWAY'S HOUSE IN BRENTWOOD is a masterful re-creation of the early California ranchos. Extending the small original cottage around the perimeter of its lot, he created a central courtyard space edged by a long veranda entwined with trumpet vines. Antique windows from Latin America, thick adobe walls, and *saltillo* floor tiles all provide a suitable background for a fine collection of Mexican and American paintings, rugs, and artifacts.

Unexpected touches, such as Chinese export porcelain and a nineteenth-century English pie-crust table, blend seamlessly into the house. "When the Europeans came here they brought European things, mixing these with primitive, more ethnic things," says Callaway, "so we were inadvertently establishing true period authenticity."

Actor Peter Horton saw Callaway's house and wanted one just like it. Callaway began by stripping back earlier remodelings of Horton's 1920s bungalow and added his favorite elements: beamed ceilings, old doors, and old windows. Horton then hung his collection of Californian plein air paintings amid layers of *retablos,* carved mirrors, Mexican Colonial furniture, and Indian blankets.

Both houses are additionally furnished with chairs designed and manufactured by Callaway and his partner, Jan Word, upholstered with leather and fabrics. They blend well with these early California–style interiors.

ABOVE: The walls by the cottage-like entry to the Callaway guest house are festooned with country roses. OPPOSITE: Mexican pots sit on a reproduction Mexican cabinet in the paved forecourt of the Callaway house. OVERLEAF LEFT: The Southwestern-style master bedroom of the Horton house (TOP), with its beamed, gently pitched ceiling, was designed and built by Callaway. Color is added by Indian rugs and blankets. The bed is flanked by Callaway-designed side tables with lamps made from Spanish Colonial candlesticks. Callaway's Niña chair is at the foot of the bed. Stable doors to the studio/guest house (BOTTOM LEFT), which occupies the rear of Callaway's garden, open onto a paved area with a Callaway-designed table. Mexican equipal chairs (BOTTOM RIGHT) surround a Callaway-designed table in the patio of the Horton house. OVERLEAF RIGHT: View into the library from the living room. The doorway is framed by a pair of retablos and country chairs from Mexico, with a Spanish-style transom window overhead. On the far wall, a California plein air painting is flanked by 1920s Italian sconces. Acoma Pueblo pots from the early 1900s line a corbeled shelf overhead. The Ernesto leather couch is by Calloway.

BIANCHI RESIDENCE

BY PENNY BIANCHI

WHILE PENNY BIANCHI, A THIRD-GENERATION Pasadena resident, was still in high school, she was invited to visit a house her mother described as the "prettiest house in Pasadena," just bought by friends of the family. For Penny, it was love at first sight, and as she was leaving, she confided to her mother, "Someday I'm going to live in this house!"

Bianchi never forgot her dream house, and eventually, through diligence and good fortune, she was able to buy it in probate. Unfortunately, by then "it looked as though the Addams family had lived there," Bianchi recalls.

Surrounded by California live oaks, the French pavilion-style house sits on the edge of the Arroyo Seco with views across to the San Gabriel Mountains. It was built in the 1950s with French panache; its complete set of bedroom paneling was rescued from an old house in Paris.

The living room is airy and generously scaled, with a large window overlooking the back terrace and the arroyo beyond. This room opens with a flourish into the dining room, with its English dining table and French fruitwood chairs. French doors, flanked by a pair of urns made in Carrara in the 1920s for Adam Bianchi's uncle, open onto a terrace. Next to the dining room is an attractive loggia with views of the arroyo and mountains.

The master bedroom is almost totally French down to the doorknobs, offering a vision of eighteenth-century Paris—except for the view outside the windows.

ABOVE: A Louis XV mirror hangs over the fireplace in the Bianchi living room. In the foreground are a pair of ottomans covered in leopardskin fabric; behind is an Austrian Biedermeier coffee table. OPPOSITE: A table is set for lunch on a covered back terrace with a sweeping view of the Pasadena arroyo and the San Gabriel mountains.

LEFT: An antique Italian pottery stove and comfortable wicker furniture decorate a loggia overlooking a peaceful French-style garden at the side of the house. ABOVE: Adam Bianchi's dressing room is furnished with a French marble fireplace, an antique child's chair, and a freestanding clothes stand. BELOW: The master bedroom is paneled in 18th-century boiserie from a chateau outside Paris. An antique Italian over-door panel hangs behind the bed.

HUTTON WILKINSON'S OWN HOUSE

SEVERAL YEARS AGO, HUTTON AND RUTH WILKINSON noticed a FOR SALE sign on an attractive 1930s Georgian Revival house and recognized it as the work of Wilkinson's architect father, Marshall Wilkinson. The house, which had been abandoned for thirty years, was bought and restored, with the help of the original architectural drawings, to good condition. "I wanted to do the house as if I were alive in 1936," said Hutton.

The Wilkinsons' love of collecting gives the house an unusual richness. Syrie Maugham's sofa, with its original ruby velvet upholstery, sits among various prizes from Elsie de Wolfe's Villa Trianon sale, as well as the De Wolfe panels, now in the entrance hall, which were found in a junk shop and identified from an old copy of *Vogue*. There are also family heirlooms, especially a collection of Colonial paintings reflecting Hutton Wilkinson's South American family background.

Wilkinson designed the living room to have "an English country house look, *à la* 1930s Elsie de Wolfe, in green and white." This gave him an opportunity to use hundreds of yards of vivid green Scalamandre brocade bought years earlier.

The back garden was landscaped by Ruth Wilkinson to create huge outdoor entertaining areas. Water cascades into the pool from a pair of Capricorn figures from the set of the film *Marie Antoinette*, which is flanked by rows of blue-and-white Oriental porcelain. "At night," says Wilkinson, "with the chandelier and candles suspended at the far end, the black-painted reflecting pool looks like a Venetian canal."

ABOVE: On a back terrace, the Wilkinsons' West Highland terrier, Jip, surveys the tiled roofscapes of 1920s Outpost Estate in the Hollywood hills. OPPOSITE: Water cascades into the pool—which is flanked by rows of blue-and-white Oriental porcelain—from a pair of Capricorn figures from the set of the film "Marie Antoinette." OVERLEAF LEFT: The sitting room is lined with Scalamandre brocade. Wilkinson decorated an 18th-century Italian mirror with pagodas and branches of coral. The draperies, made of plaster-dipped fabric, were a housewarming gift from Tony Duquette. OVERLEAF RIGHT: The sitting-room fireplace (TOP LEFT) is capped by a16th-century Italian painting and flanked by two Chinese cloisonné cranes. The chairs, upholstered in malachite fabric, appeared in MGM's "The Thin Man." Nineteenth-century vues optiques prints (TOP LEFT) line the walls in a quiet corner of the sitting room. The chairs are 19th-century French. The entry hall, with two Elsie de Wolfe painted panels (BOTTOM RIGHT). Wilkinson stippled the walls and ceiling, the latter with a sky effect to generate an effect of height. Wilkinson calls the white pine-paneled dining room (BOTTOM RIGHT) "a room of pleasure palaces." Its walls are hung with 19th-century prints of Brighton Pavilion by John Nash and 18th-century Chinese prints of pleasure palaces in China.

ABOVE: In a corner of the deal-paneled library, a painting from Georgia of a princess hangs over a Syrie Maugham couch—made for the actress Ina Claire—with its original ruby velvet upholstery. ABOVE RIGHT: A desk filled with family photographs is framed by puce-colored silk taffeta curtains. In front is a brown suede-covered rattan-backed Louis XV chair. RIGHT: A canopied bed, which appeared in "The Thin Man," and a coral silk-upholstered couch rest on a First Empire Aubusson carpet. Behind is a 1920s Chinese screen. OPPOSITE: The 17th-century Venetian dressing table with a 1930s blue lacquer finish is from the estate of Elsie de Wolfe. "Rothschild-style" bronze oil lamps from the 19th century are placed on either side of a Victorian mirror and family mementos. Eighteenth-century Italian paintings of the seasons flank a 17th-century Colonial painting of a cavalier saint.

INDEX